# FRENCH

## Grammar

Besonde
J'ai envie de
Je voudrais

CollinsGem

*An Imprint of* HarperCollins*Publishers*

third edition 2001
first published in this format 2003

**latest reprint 2003**

HarperCollins Publishers
Westerhill Road, Bishopbriggs, Glasgow G64 2QT
Great Britain

ISBN 0-00-716258-8

**www.collinsdictionaries.com**

The HarperCollins USA website address is
www.harpercollins.com

Lesley A Robertson • Lorna Sinclair

*editorial staff*
Christine Penman, Megan Thomson

*editorial management*
Vivian Marr

A catalogue record for this book is available
from the British Library

Typeset by Ruth Noble, Peebles

Printed and bound in Italy by Amadeus S.p.A.

# INTRODUCTION

The **Collins Gem French Grammar** is designed to offer students of French of all ages and at all levels an uncluttered, step-by-step guide to the grammar of the language. For the person with little or no knowledge of French it provides the basic 'tools' necessary for comprehension and communication, and for the more advanced learner it provides an efficient and speedy means of reference and revision.

As you will see from the contents list overleaf, the book is split into sections according to part of speech (nouns, articles, adjectives etc) or grammar point (sentence structure, use of numbers etc). As far as is possible, we have tried to anticipate any grammatical terms with which you may not be familiar, and a brief explanation is given at the relevant point in the text.

A special feature of this book is the clear demarcation of grammatical points, each of which is treated on a left-hand page and illustrated by numerous practical, up-to-date examples on the opposite right-hand page. For instance, turn to page 154 and you will see a series of boxed numbers → [1] to → [10] throughout the text on that page. These numbers cross-refer you to an example, or group of examples, on page 155. This double-page layout gives you maximum accessibility to the grammar point you want to learn or revise, while the examples help fix that grammar point firmly in your mind.

Special attention is paid throughout the book to potential problem areas – such as sentence structure, where French usage can differ markedly from English usage. In addition, the section on translation problems alerts you to some of the most common pitfalls of translation. A full index, with both grammatical topics and key words in French and English, completes the grammar.

## ABBREVIATIONS

| | | | | | |
|---|---|---|---|---|---|
| **ctd.** | continued | **p(p)** | page(s) | **qn** | quelqu'un |
| **fem.** | feminine | **perf.** | perfect | **sb** | somebody |
| **infin.** | infinitive | **plur.** | plural | **sing.** | singular |
| **masc.** | masculine | **qch** | quelque chose | **sth** | something |

# CONTENTS

# CONTENTS

## ❏ Simple Tenses: formation

In French the simple tenses are:

| | |
|---|---|
| Present | → ① |
| Imperfect | → ② |
| Future | → ③ |
| Conditional | → ④ |
| Past Historic | → ⑤ |
| Present Subjunctive | → ⑥ |
| Imperfect Subjunctive | → ⑦ |

They are formed by adding endings to a verb stem. The endings show the number and person of the subject of the verb → ⑧

The stem and endings of regular verbs are totally predictable. The following sections show all the patterns for regular verbs. For irregular verbs see pp 74 ff.

## ❏ Regular Verbs

There are three regular verb patterns (called conjugations), each identifiable by the ending of the infinitive:

- First conjugation verbs end in **-er** e.g. **donner** to give
- Second conjugation verbs end in **-ir** e.g. **finir** to finish
- Third conjugation verbs end in **-re** e.g. **vendre** to sell

These three conjugations are treated in order on the following pages.

| | | |
|---|---|---|
| 1 | **je donne** | I give<br>I am giving<br>I do give |
| 2 | **je donnais** | I gave<br>I was giving<br>I used to give |
| 3 | **je donnerai** | I shall give<br>I shall be giving |
| 4 | **je donnerais** | I should/would give<br>I should/would be giving |
| 5 | **je donnai** | I gave |
| 6 | **(que) je donne** | (that) I give/gave |
| 7 | **(que) je donnasse** | (that) I gave |
| 8 | **je donne**<br>**nous donnons**<br>**je donnerais**<br>**nous donnerions** | I give<br>we give<br>I would give<br>we would give |

## ❑ Simple Tenses: First Conjugation

+ The stem is formed as follows:

| TENSE | FORMATION | EXAMPLE |
|---|---|---|
| Present<br>Imperfect<br>Past Historic<br>Present Subjunctive<br>Imperfect Subjunctive | infinitive minus **-er** | **donn-** |
| Future<br>Conditional | infinitive | **donner-** |

+ To the appropriate stem add the following endings:

| | | PRESENT<br>→ ① | IMPERFECT<br>→ ② | PAST HISTORIC<br>→ ③ |
|---|---|---|---|---|
| sing. | 1st person | -e | -ais | -ai |
| | 2nd person | -es | -ais | -as |
| | 3rd person | -e | -ait | -a |
| plur. | 1st person | -ons | -ions | -âmes |
| | 2nd person | -ez | -iez | -âtes |
| | 3rd person | -ent | -aient | -èrent |

| | | PRESENT<br>SUBJUNCTIVE → ④ | IMPERFECT<br>SUBJUNCTIVE → ⑤ |
|---|---|---|---|
| sing. | 1st person | -e | -asse |
| | 2nd person | -es | -asses |
| | 3rd person | -e | -ât |
| plur. | 1st person | -ions | -assions |
| | 2nd person | -iez | -assiez |
| | 3rd person | -ent | -assent |

| | | FUTURE → ⑥ | CONDITIONAL → ⑦ |
|---|---|---|---|
| sing. | 1st person | -ai | -ais |
| | 2nd person | -as | -ais |
| | 3rd person | -a | -ait |
| plur. | 1st person | -ons | -ions |
| | 2nd person | -ez | -iez |
| | 3rd person | -ont | -aient |

# Examples

**1 PRESENT**

| je | donne |
| tu | donnes |
| il | donne |
| elle | donne |
| nous | donnons |
| vous | donnez |
| ils | donnent |
| elles | donnent |

**2 IMPERFECT**

| je | donnais |
| tu | donnais |
| il | donnait |
| elle | donnait |
| nous | donnions |
| vous | donniez |
| ils | donnaient |
| elles | donnaient |

**3 PAST HISTORIC**

| je | donnai |
| tu | donnas |
| il | donna |
| elle | donna |
| nous | donnâmes |
| vous | donnâtes |
| ils | donnèrent |
| elles | donnèrent |

**4 PRESENT SUBJUNCTIVE**

| je | donne |
| tu | donnes |
| il | donne |
| elle | donne |
| nous | donnions |
| vous | donniez |
| ils | donnent |
| elles | donnent |

**5 IMPERFECT SUBJUNCTIVE**

| je | donnasse |
| tu | donnasses |
| il | donnât |
| elle | donnât |
| nous | donnassions |
| vous | donnassiez |
| ils | donnassent |
| elles | donnassent |

**6 FUTURE**

| je | donnerai |
| tu | donneras |
| il | donnera |
| elle | donnera |
| nous | donnerons |
| vous | donnerez |
| ils | donneront |
| elles | donneront |

**7 CONDITIONAL**

| je | donnerais |
| tu | donnerais |
| il | donnerait |
| elle | donnerait |
| nous | donnerions |
| vous | donneriez |
| ils | donneraient |
| elles | donneraient |

## □ Simple Tenses: Second Conjugation

• The stem is formed as follows:

| TENSE | FORMATION | EXAMPLE |
|---|---|---|
| Present | | |
| Imperfect | | |
| Past Historic | infinitive minus -ir | fin- |
| Present Subjunctive | | |
| Imperfect Subjunctive | | |
| Future | infinitive | finir- |
| Conditional | | |

• To the appropriate stem add the following endings:

| | | PRESENT → [1] | IMPERFECT → [2] | PAST HISTORIC → [3] |
|---|---|---|---|---|
| sing. | 1st person | -is | -issais | -is |
| | 2nd person | -is | -issais | -is |
| | 3rd person | -it | -issait | -it |
| plur. | 1st person | -issons | -issions | -îmes |
| | 2nd person | -issez | -issiez | -îtes |
| | 3rd person | -issent | -issaient | -irent |

| | | PRESENT SUBJUNCTIVE → [4] | IMPERFECT SUBJUNCTIVE → [5] |
|---|---|---|---|
| sing. | 1st person | -isse | -isse |
| | 2nd person | -isses | -isses |
| | 3rd person | -isse | -ît |
| plur. | 1st person | -issions | -issions |
| | 2nd person | -issiez | -issiez |
| | 3rd person | -issent | -issent |

| | | FUTURE → [6] | CONDITIONAL → [7] |
|---|---|---|---|
| sing. | 1st person | -ai | -ais |
| | 2nd person | -as | -ais |
| | 3rd person | -a | -ait |
| plur. | 1st person | -ons | -ions |
| | 2nd person | -ez | -iez |
| | 3rd person | -ont | -aient |

# Examples

Grammar

| | [1] PRESENT | | [2] IMPERFECT | | [3] PAST HISTORIC |
|---|---|---|---|---|---|
| je | finis | je | finissais | je | finis |
| tu | finis | tu | finissais | tu | finis |
| il | finit | il | finissait | il | finit |
| elle | finit | elle | finissait | elle | finit |
| nous | finissons | nous | finissions | nous | finîmes |
| vous | finissez | vous | finissiez | vous | finîtes |
| ils | finissent | ils | finissaient | ils | finirent |
| elles | finissent | elles | finissaient | elles | finirent |

| | [4] PRESENT SUBJUNCTIVE | | [5] IMPERFECT SUBJUNCTIVE |
|---|---|---|---|
| je | finisse | je | finisse |
| tu | finisses | tu | finisses |
| il | finisse | il | finît |
| elle | finisse | elle | finît |
| nous | finissions | nous | finissions |
| vous | finissiez | vous | finissiez |
| ils | finissent | ils | finissent |
| elles | finissent | elles | finissent |

| | [6] FUTURE | | [7] CONDITIONAL |
|---|---|---|---|
| je | finirai | je | finirais |
| tu | finiras | tu | finirais |
| il | finira | il | finirait |
| elle | finira | elle | finirait |
| nous | finirons | nous | finirions |
| vous | finirez | vous | finiriez |
| ils | finiront | ils | finiraient |
| elles | finiront | elles | finiraient |

## ❒ Simple Tenses: Third Conjugation

• The stem is formed as follows:

| TENSE | FORMATION | EXAMPLE |
|---|---|---|
| Present<br>Imperfect<br>Past Historic<br>Present Subjunctive<br>Imperfect Subjunctive | infinitive minus **-re** | **vend-** |
| Future<br>Conditional | infinitive minus **-e** | **vendr-** |

• To the appropriate stem add the following endings:

|  |  | PRESENT<br>→ 1 | IMPERFECT<br>→ 2 | PAST HISTORIC<br>→ 3 |
|---|---|---|---|---|
| sing. | 1st person | -s | -ais | -is |
|  | 2nd person | -s | -ais | -is |
|  | 3rd person | – | -ait | -it |
| plur. | 1st person | -ons | -ions | -îmes |
|  | 2nd person | -ez | -iez | -îtes |
|  | 3rd person | -ent | -aient | -irent |

|  |  | PRESENT<br>SUBJUNCTIVE → 4 | IMPERFECT<br>SUBJUNCTIVE → 5 |
|---|---|---|---|
| sing. | 1st person | -e | -isse |
|  | 2nd person | -es | -isses |
|  | 3rd person | -e | -ît |
| plur. | 1st person | -ions | -issions |
|  | 2nd person | -iez | -issiez |
|  | 3rd person | -ent | -issent |

|  |  | FUTURE → 6 | CONDITIONAL → 7 |
|---|---|---|---|
| sing. | 1st person | -ai | -ais |
|  | 2nd person | -as | -ais |
|  | 3rd person | -a | -ait |
| plur. | 1st person | -ons | -ions |
|  | 2nd person | -ez | -iez |
|  | 3rd person | -ont | -aient |

Grammar

| | **1 PRESENT** | | **2 IMPERFECT** | | **3 PAST HISTORIC** |
|---|---|---|---|---|---|
| je | vend**s** | je | vend**ais** | je | vend**is** |
| tu | vend**s** | tu | vend**ais** | tu | vend**is** |
| il | vend | il | vend**ait** | il | vend**it** |
| elle | vend | elle | vend**ait** | elle | vend**it** |
| nous | vend**ons** | nous | vend**ions** | nous | vend**îmes** |
| vous | vend**ez** | vous | vend**iez** | vous | vend**îtes** |
| ils | vend**ent** | ils | vend**aient** | ils | vend**irent** |
| elles | vend**ent** | elles | vend**aient** | elles | vend**irent** |

| | **4 PRESENT SUBJUNCTIVE** | | **5 IMPERFECT SUBJUNCTIVE** |
|---|---|---|---|
| je | vend**e** | je | vend**isse** |
| tu | vend**es** | tu | vend**isses** |
| il | vend**e** | il | vend**ît** |
| elle | vend**e** | elle | vend**ît** |
| nous | vend**ions** | nous | vend**issions** |
| vous | vend**iez** | vous | vend**issiez** |
| ils | vend**ent** | ils | vend**issent** |
| elles | vend**ent** | elles | vend**issent** |

| | **6 FUTURE** | | **7 CONDITIONAL** |
|---|---|---|---|
| je | vend**rai** | je | vend**rais** |
| tu | vend**ras** | tu | vend**rais** |
| il | vend**ra** | il | vend**rait** |
| elle | vend**ra** | elle | vend**rait** |
| nous | vend**rons** | nous | vend**rions** |
| vous | vend**rez** | vous | vend**riez** |
| ils | vend**ront** | ils | vend**raient** |
| elles | vend**ront** | elles | vend**raient** |

## ❏ First Conjugation Spelling Irregularities

Before certain endings, the stems of some '-er' verbs may change slightly.

Below, and on subsequent pages, the verb types are identified, and the changes described are illustrated by means of a representative verb.

| | |
|---|---|
| Verbs ending: | **-cer** |
| Change: | **c** becomes **ç** before **a** or **o** |
| Tenses affected: | Present, Imperfect, Past Historic, Imperfect Subjunctive, Present Participle |
| Model: | **lancer** *to throw* → 1 |

◆ Why the change occurs:
   A cedilla is added to the **c** to retain its soft [s] pronunciation before the vowels **a** and **o**.

| | |
|---|---|
| Verbs ending: | **-ger** |
| Change: | **g** becomes **ge** before **a** or **o** |
| Tenses affected: | Present, Imperfect, Past Historic, Imperfect Subjunctive, Present Participle |
| Model: | **manger** *to eat* → 2 |

◆ Why the change occurs:
   An **e** is added after the **g** to retain its soft [ʒ] pronunciation before the vowels **a** and **o**.

| | | |
|---|---|---|
| **1** INFINITIVE | | PRESENT PARTICIPLE |
| **lancer** | | **lançant** |

| PRESENT | | IMPERFECT | |
|---|---|---|---|
| je | lance | **je** | **lançais** |
| tu | lances | **tu** | **lançais** |
| il/elle | lance | **il/elle** | **lançait** |
| **nous** | **lançons** | nous | lancions |
| vous | lancez | vous | lanciez |
| ils/elles | lancent | **ils/elles** | **lançaient** |

| PAST HISTORIC | | IMPERFECT SUBJUNCTIVE | |
|---|---|---|---|
| **je** | **lançai** | **je** | **lançasse** |
| **tu** | **lanças** | **tu** | **lançasses** |
| **il/elle** | **lança** | **il/elle** | **lançât** |
| **nous** | **lançâmes** | **nous** | **lançassions** |
| **vous** | **lançâtes** | **vous** | **lançassiez** |
| ils/elles | lancèrent | **ils/elles** | **lançassent** |

| | | |
|---|---|---|
| **2** INFINITIVE | | PRESENT PARTICIPLE |
| **manger** | | **mangeant** |

| PRESENT | | IMPERFECT | |
|---|---|---|---|
| je | mange | **je** | **mangeais** |
| tu | manges | **tu** | **mangeais** |
| il/elle | mange | **il/elle** | **mangeait** |
| **nous** | **mangeons** | nous | mangions |
| vous | mangez | vous | mangiez |
| ils/elles | mangent | **ils/elles** | **mangeaient** |

| PAST HISTORIC | | IMPERFECT SUBJUNCTIVE | |
|---|---|---|---|
| **je** | **mangeai** | **je** | **mangeasse** |
| **tu** | **mangeas** | **tu** | **mangeasses** |
| **il/elle** | **mangea** | **il/elle** | **mangeât** |
| **nous** | **mangeâmes** | **nous** | **mangeassions** |
| **vous** | **mangeâtes** | **vous** | **mangeassiez** |
| ils/elles | mangèrent | **ils/elles** | **mangeassent** |

## ▢ First Conjugation Spelling Irregularities *(Continued)*

| | |
|---|---|
| Verbs ending | **-eler** |
| Change: | **-l** doubles before **-e**, **-es**, **-ent** and throughout the Future and Conditional tenses |
| Tenses affected: | Present, Present Subjunctive, Future, Conditional |
| Model: | **appeler** *to call* → ① |

◆ EXCEPTIONS: **geler** *to freeze* } like **mener** (p 18)
          **peler** *to peel*

| | |
|---|---|
| Verbs ending | **-eter** |
| Change: | **-t** doubles before **-e**, **-es**, **-ent** and throughout the Future and Conditional tenses |
| Tenses affected: | Present, Present Subjunctive, Future, Conditional |
| Model: | **jeter** *to throw* → ② |

◆ EXCEPTIONS: **acheter** *to buy* } like **mener** (p 18)
          **haleter** *to pant*

| | |
|---|---|
| Verbs ending | **-yer** |
| Change: | **y** changes to **i** before **-e**, **-es**, **-ent** and throughout the Future and Conditional tenses |
| Tenses affected: | Present, Present Subjunctive, Future, Conditional |
| Model: | **essuyer** *to wipe* → ③ |

◆ The change described is optional for verbs ending in **-ayer** e.g. **payer** *to pay*, **essayer** *to try*.

| | **1** PRESENT (+ SUBJUNCTIVE) | FUTURE |
|---|---|---|
| | **j'appelle** | **j'appellerai** |
| **tu** | **appelles** | **tu appelleras** |
| **il/elle** | **appelle** | **il appellera** *etc* |
| nous | appelons | |
| | (appelions) | CONDITIONAL |
| vous | appelez | **j'appellerais** |
| | (appeliez) | **tu appellerais** |
| **ils/elles** | **appellent** | **il appellerait** *etc* |

| | **2** PRESENT (+ SUBJUNCTIVE) | FUTURE |
|---|---|---|
| **je** | **jette** | **je jetterai** |
| **tu** | **jettes** | **tu jetteras** |
| **il/elle** | **jette** | **il jettera** *etc* |
| nous | jetons | |
| | (jetions) | CONDITIONAL |
| vous | jetez | **je jetterais** |
| | (jetiez) | **tu jetterais** |
| **ils/elles** | **jettent** | **il jetterait** *etc* |

| | **3** PRESENT (+ SUBJUNCTIVE) | FUTURE |
|---|---|---|
| | **j'essuie** | **j'essuierai** |
| **tu** | **essuies** | **tu essuieras** |
| **il/elle** | **essuie** | **il essuiera** *etc* |
| nous | essuyons | |
| | (essuyions) | CONDITIONAL |
| vous | essuyez | **j'essuierais** |
| | (essuyiez) | **tu essuierais** |
| **ils/elles** | **essuient** | **il essuierait** *etc* |

*Grammar*

## ☐ First Conjugation Spelling Irregularities *(Continued)*

| | |
|---|---|
| Verbs ending | **mener, peser, lever** *etc* |
| Change: | **e** changes to **è**, before **-e, -es, -ent** and throughout the Future and Conditional tenses |
| Tenses affected: | Present, Present Subjunctive, Future, Conditional |
| Model: | **mener** *to lead* → ① |

| | |
|---|---|
| Verbs like: | **céder, régler, espérer** *etc* |
| Change: | **é** changes to **è** before **-e, -es, -ent** |
| Tenses affected: | Present, Present Subjunctive |
| Model: | **céder** *to yield* → ② |

# Examples

**1 PRESENT (+ SUBJUNCTIVE)**

| | | | |
|---|---|---|---|
| je | **mène** | | |
| tu | **mènes** | | |
| il/elle | **mène** | | |
| nous | menons | | |
| | (menions) | | |
| vous | menez | | |
| | (meniez) | | |
| **ils/elles** | **mènent** | | |

**FUTURE**

| | |
|---|---|
| je | **mènerai** |
| tu | **mèneras** |
| il | **mènera** *etc* |

**CONDITIONAL**

| | |
|---|---|
| je | **mènerais** |
| tu | **mènerais** |
| il | **mènerait** *etc* |

**2 PRESENT (+ SUBJUNCTIVE)**

| | |
|---|---|
| je | **cède** |
| tu | **cèdes** |
| il/elle | **cède** |
| nous | cédons |
| | (cédions) |
| vous | cédez |
| | (cédiez) |
| **ils/elles** | **cèdent** |

## ◻ The Imperative

The imperative is the form of the verb used to give commands or orders. It can be used politely, as in English 'Shut the door, please'.

The imperative is the same as the present tense **tu, nous** and **vous** forms without the subject pronouns:

| **donne\*** | **finis** | **vends** |
|---|---|---|
| *give* | *finish* | *sell* |

\*The final 's' of the present tense of first conjugation verbs is dropped, except before **y** and **en** → ①

| **donnons** | **finissons** | **vendons** |
|---|---|---|
| *let's give* | *let's finish* | *let's sell* |

| **donnez** | **finissez** | **vendez** |
|---|---|---|
| *give* | *finish* | *sell* |

+ The imperative of irregular verbs is given in the verb tables, pp 74 ff.

+ Position of object pronouns with the imperative:
  in POSITIVE commands: they follow the verb and are attached to it by hyphens → ②
  in NEGATIVE commands: they precede the verb and are not attached to it → ③

+ For the order of object pronouns, see p 170.

+ For reflexive verbs – e.g. **se lever** *to get up* – the object pronoun is the reflexive pronoun → ④

# Examples

1. Compare: **Tu donnes de l'argent à Paul**
   You give (some) money to Paul
   and: **Donne de l'argent à Paul**
   Give (some) money to Paul

2. **Excusez-moi**
   Excuse me
   **Crois-nous**
   Believe us
   **Attendons-la**
   Let's wait for her/it

   **Envoyons-les-leur**
   Let's send them to them
   **Expliquez-le-moi**
   Explain it to me
   **Rends-la-lui**
   Give it back to him/her

3. **Ne me dérange pas**
   Don't disturb me
   **Ne les négligeons pas**
   Let's not neglect them
   **Ne leur répondez pas**
   Don't answer them

   **Ne leur en parlons pas**
   Let's not speak to them about it
   **N'y pense plus**
   Don't think about it any more
   **Ne la lui rends pas**
   Don't give it back to him/her

4. **Lève-toi**
   Get up
   **Dépêchons-nous**
   Let's hurry
   **Levez-vous**
   Get up

   **Ne te lève pas**
   Don't get up
   **Ne nous affolons pas**
   Let's not panic
   **Ne vous levez pas**
   Don't get up

## ❏ Compound Tenses: formation

In French the compound tenses are:

| | |
|---|---|
| Perfect | → 1 |
| Pluperfect | → 2 |
| Future Perfect | → 3 |
| Conditional Perfect | → 4 |
| Past Anterior | → 5 |
| Perfect Subjunctive | → 6 |
| Pluperfect Subjunctive | → 7 |

They consist of the past participle of the verb together with an auxiliary verb. Most verbs take the auxiliary **avoir**, but some take **être** (see p 28).

Compound tenses are formed in exactly the same way for both regular and irregular verbs, the only difference being that irregular verbs may have an irregular past participle.

## ❏ The Past Participle

For all compound tenses you need to know how to form the past participle of the verb. For regular verbs this is as follows:

◆ 1st conjugation: replace the **-er** of the infinitive by **-é** → 8

◆ 2nd conjugation: replace the **-ir** of the infinitive by **-i** → 9

◆ 3rd conjugation: replace the **-re** of the infinitive by **-u** → 10

◆ See p 50 for agreement of past participles.

| with **avoir** | with **être** |
|---|---|

1. **j'ai donné**
I gave, have given

    **je suis tombé**
I fell, have fallen

2. **j'avais donné**
I had given

    **j'étais tombé**
I had fallen

3. **j'aurai donné**
I shall have given

    **je serai tombé**
I shall have fallen

4. **j'aurais donné**
I should /would have given

    **je serais tombé**
I should/would have fallen

5. **j'eus donné**
I had given

    **je fus tombé**
I had fallen

6. **(que) j'aie donné**
(that) I gave, have given

    **(que) je sois tombé**
(that) I fell, have fallen

7. **(que) j'eusse donné**
(that) I had given

    **(que) je fusse tombé**
(that) I had fallen

8. **donner** → **donné**
to give     given

9. **finir** → **fini**
to finish    finished

10. **vendre** → **vendu**
to sell     sold

## ◻ Compound Tenses: formation *(Continued)*

### Verbs taking the auxiliary avoir

| | |
|---|---|
| Perfect tense: | the present tense of **avoir** plus the past participle → 1 |
| Pluperfect tense: | the imperfect tense of **avoir** plus the past participle → 2 |
| Future Perfect: | the future tense of **avoir** plus the past participle → 3 |
| Conditional Perfect: | the conditional of **avoir** plus the past participle → 4 |
| Past Anterior: | the past historic of **avoir** plus the past participle → 5 |
| Perfect Subjunctive: | the present subjunctive of **avoir** plus the past participle → 6 |
| Pluperfect Subjunctive: | the imperfect subjunctive of **avoir** plus the past participle → 7 |

◆ For how to form the past participle of regular verbs see p 22. The past participle of irregular verbs is given for each verb in the verb tables, pp 74 ff.

◆ The past participle must agree in number and in gender with any preceding direct object (see p 50).

# Examples

☐1 PERFECT

| j'ai donné | nous avons donné |
| tu as donné | vous avez donné |
| il/elle a donné | ils/elles ont donné |

☐2 PLUPERFECT

| j'avais donné | nous avions donné |
| tu avais donné | vous aviez donné |
| il/elle avait donné | ils/elles avaient donné |

☐3 FUTURE PERFECT

| j'aurai donné | nous aurons donné |
| tu auras donné | vous aurez donné |
| il/elle aura donné | ils/elles auront donné |

☐4 CONDITIONAL PERFECT

| j'aurais donné | nous aurions donné |
| tu aurais donné | vous auriez donné |
| il/elle aurait donné | ils/elles auraient donné |

☐5 PAST ANTERIOR

| j'eus donné | nous eûmes donné |
| tu eus donné | vous eûtes donné |
| il/elle eut donné | ils/elles eurent donné |

☐6 PERFECT SUBJUNCTIVE

| j'aie donné | nous ayons donné |
| tu aies donné | vous ayez donné |
| il/elle ait donné | ils/elles aient donné |

☐7 PLUPERFECT SUBJUNCTIVE

| j'eusse donné | nous eussions donné |
| tu eusses donné | vous eussiez donné |
| il/elle eût donné | ils/elles eussent donné |

## ◻ Compound Tenses: formation *(Continued)*

### Verbs taking the auxiliary être

| | |
|---|---|
| Perfect tense: | the present tense of **être** plus the past participle → ☐1 |
| Pluperfect tense: | the imperfect tense of **être** plus the past participle → ☐2 |
| Future Perfect: | the future tense of **être** plus the past participle → ☐3 |
| Conditional Perfect: | the conditional of **être** plus the past participle → ☐4 |
| Past Anterior: | the past historic of **être** plus the past participle → ☐5 |
| Perfect Subjunctive: | the present subjunctive of **être** plus the past participle → ☐6 |
| Pluperfect Subjunctive: | the imperfect subjunctive of **être** plus the past participle → ☐7 |

+ For how to form the past participle of regular verbs see p 22. The past participle of irregular verbs is given for each verb in the verb tables, pp 74 ff.

+ For agreement of past participles, see p 50.

+ For a list of verbs and verb types that take the auxiliary **être**, see p 28.

# Examples

**1 PERFECT**

| | |
|---|---|
| je suis tombé(e) | nous sommes tombé(e)s |
| tu es tombé(e) | vous êtes tombé(e)(s) |
| il est tombé | ils sont tombés |
| elle est tombée | elles sont tombées |

**2 PLUPERFECT**

| | |
|---|---|
| j'étais tombé(e) | nous étions tombé(e)s |
| tu étais tombé(e) | vous étiez tombé(e)(s) |
| il était tombé | ils étaient tombés |
| elle était tombée | elles étaient tombées |

**3 FUTURE PERFECT**

| | |
|---|---|
| je serai tombé(e) | nous serons tombé(e)s |
| tu seras tombé(e) | vous serez tombé(e)(s) |
| il sera tombé | ils seront tombés |
| elle sera tombée | elles seront tombées |

**4 CONDITIONAL PERFECT**

| | |
|---|---|
| je serais tombé(e) | nous serions tombé(e)s |
| tu serais tombé(e) | vous seriez tombé(e)(s) |
| il serait tombé | ils seraient tombés |
| elle serait tombée | elles seraient tombées |

**5 PAST ANTERIOR**

| | |
|---|---|
| je fus tombé(e) | nous fûmes tombé(e)s |
| tu fus tombé(e) | vous fûtes tombé(e)(s) |
| il fut tombé | ils furent tombés |
| elle fut tombée | elles furent tombées |

**6 PERFECT SUBJUNCTIVE**

| | |
|---|---|
| je sois tombé(e) | nous soyons tombé(e)s |
| tu sois tombé(e) | vous soyez tombé(e)(s) |
| il soit tombé | ils soient tombés |
| elle soit tombée | elles soient tombées |

**7 PLUPERFECT SUBJUNCTIVE**

| | |
|---|---|
| je fusse tombé(e) | nous fussions tombé(e)s |
| tu fusses tombé(e) | vous fussiez tombé(e)(s) |
| il fût tombé | ils fussent tombés |
| elle fût tombée | elles fussent tombées |

## ❏ Compound Tenses *(Continued)*

### The following verbs take the auxiliary être

◆ Reflexive verbs (see p 30) → 1

◆ The following intransitive verbs (i.e. verbs which cannot take a direct object), largely expressing motion or a change of state:

| | | | |
|---|---|---|---|
| **aller** | *to go* → 2 | **passer** | *to pass* |
| **arriver** | *to arrive; to happen* | **rentrer** | *to go back/in* |
| **descendre** | *to go/come down* | **rester** | *to stay* → 5 |
| **devenir** | *to become* | **retourner** | *to go back* |
| **entrer** | *to go/come in* | **revenir** | *to come back* |
| **monter** | *to go/come up* | **sortir** | *to go/come out* |
| **mourir** | *to die* → 3 | **tomber** | *to fall* |
| **naître** | *to be born* | **venir** | *to come* → 6 |
| **partir** | *to leave* → 4 | | |

◆ Of these, the following are conjugated with **avoir** when used transitively (i.e. with a direct object):

| | |
|---|---|
| **descendre** | *to bring/take down* |
| **entrer** | *to bring/take in* |
| **monter** | *to bring/take up* → 7 |
| **passer** | *to pass; to spend* → 8 |
| **rentrer** | *to bring/take in* |
| **retourner** | *to turn over* |
| **sortir** | *to bring/take out* → 9 |

⚠ NOTE that the past participle must show an agreement in number and gender whenever the auxiliary is **être** EXCEPT FOR REFLEXIVE VERBS WHERE THE REFLEXIVE PRONOUN IS THE INDIRECT OBJECT (see p 50).

☐1 **je me suis arrêté(e)**
I stopped
**tu t'es levé(e)**
you got up

**elle s'est trompée**
she made a mistake
**ils s'étaient battus**
they had fought (one another)

☐2 **elle est allée**
she went

☐3 **ils sont morts**
they died

☐4 **vous êtes partie**
you left *(addressing a female person)*
**vous êtes parties**
you left *(addressing more than one female person)*

☐5 **nous sommes resté(e)s**
we stayed

☐6 **elles étaient venues**
they [female] had come

☐7 **Il a monté les valises**
He's taken up the cases

☐8 **Nous avons passé trois semaines chez elle**
We spent three weeks at her place

☐9 **Avez-vous sorti la voiture?**
Have you taken the car out?

## ◻ Reflexive Verbs

A reflexive verb is one accompanied by a reflexive pronoun, e.g. **se lever** *to get up*; **se laver** *to wash (oneself)*. The pronouns are:

| PERSON | SINGULAR | PLURAL |
|--------|----------|--------|
| 1st | **me (m')** | **nous** |
| 2nd | **te (t')** | **vous** |
| 3rd | **se (s')** | **se (s')** |

The forms shown in brackets are used before a vowel, an **h** 'mute', or the pronoun **y** → ①

◆ In positive commands, **te** changes to **toi** → ②

◆ The reflexive pronoun 'reflects back' to the subject, but it is not always translated in English → ③

The plural pronouns are sometimes translated as *one another, each other* (the 'reciprocal' meaning) → ④

The reciprocal meaning may be emphasized by **l'un(e) l'autre (les un(e)s les autres)** → ⑤

◆ Simple tenses of reflexive verbs are conjugated in exactly the same way as those of non-reflexive verbs except that the reflexive pronoun is always used. Compound tenses are formed with the auxiliary **être**. A sample reflexive verb is conjugated in full on pp 34 and 35.

For agreement of past participles, see p 32.

### Position of Reflexive Pronouns

◆ In constructions other than the imperative affirmative the pronoun comes before the verb → ⑥

◆ In the imperative affirmative, the pronoun follows the verb and is attached to it by a hyphen → ⑦

# Examples

**Grammar**

1. **Je m'ennuie**
   I'm bored
   **Elle s'habille**
   She's getting dressed
   **Ils s'y intéressent**
   They are interested in it

2. **Assieds-toi**
   Sit down
   **Tais-toi**
   Be quiet

3. **Je me prépare**
   I'm getting (myself) ready
   **Nous nous lavons**
   We're washing (ourselves)
   **Elle se lève**
   She gets up

4. **Nous nous parlons**
   We speak to each other
   **Ils se ressemblent**
   They resemble one another

5. **Ils se regardent l'un l'autre**
   They are looking at each other

6. **Je me couche tôt**
   I go to bed early
   **Comment vous appelez-vous?**
   What is your name?
   **Il ne s'est pas rasé**
   He hasn't shaved
   **Ne te dérange pas pour nous**
   Don't put yourself out on our account

7. **Dépêche-toi**
   Hurry (up)
   **Renseignons-nous**
   Let's find out
   **Asseyez-vous**
   Sit down

## ❑ Reflexive Verbs *(Continued)*

### Past Participle Agreement

- In most reflexive verbs the reflexive pronoun is a DIRECT object pronoun → ①

- When a direct object accompanies the reflexive verb the pronoun is then the INDIRECT object → ②

- The past participle of a reflexive verb agrees in number and gender with a direct object which *precedes* the verb (usually, but not always, the reflexive pronoun) → ③

  The past participle does not change if the direct object follows the verb → ④

Here are some common reflexive verbs:

| | | | |
|---|---|---|---|
| s'en aller | *to go away* | se hâter | *to hurry* |
| s'amuser | *to enjoy oneself* | se laver | *to wash (oneself)* |
| s'appeler | *to be called* | se lever | *to get up* |
| s'arrêter | *to stop* | se passer | *to happen* |
| s'asseoir | *to sit (down)* | se promener | *to go for a walk* |
| se baigner | *to go swimming* | se rappeler | *to remember* |
| se blesser | *to hurt oneself* | se ressembler | *to resemble each other* |
| se coucher | *to go to bed* | se retourner | *to turn round* |
| se demander | *to wonder* | se réveiller | *to wake up* |
| se dépêcher | *to hurry* | se sauver | *to run away* |
| se diriger | *to make one's way* | se souvenir de | *to remember* |
| s'endormir | *to fall asleep* | se taire | *to be quiet* |
| s'ennuyer | *to be/get bored* | se tromper | *to be mistaken* |
| se fâcher | *to get angry* | se trouver | *to be (situated)* |
| s'habiller | *to dress (oneself)* | | |

1. **Je m'appelle**
I'm called *(literally: I call myself)*
**Asseyez-vous**
Sit down *(literally: Seat yourself)*
**Ils se lavent**
They wash (themselves)

2. **Elle se lave les mains**
She's washing her hands *(literally: She's washing to herself the hands)*
**Je me brosse les dents**
I brush my teeth
**Nous nous envoyons des cadeaux à Noël**
We send presents to each other at Christmas

3. **'Je me suis endormi' s'est-il excusé**
'I fell asleep', he apologized
**Pauline s'est dirigée vers la sortie**
Pauline made her way towards the exit
**Ils se sont levés vers dix heures**
They got up around ten o'clock
**Elles se sont excusées de leur erreur**
They apologized for their mistake
**Est-ce que tu t'es blessée, Cécile?**
Have you hurt yourself, Cécile?

4. **Elle s'est lavé les cheveux**
She (has) washed her hair
**Nous nous sommes serré la main**
We shook hands
**Christine s'est cassé la jambe**
Christine has broken her leg

◻ **Reflexive Verbs** *(Continued)*

Conjugation of: **se laver** *to wash (oneself)*

---

**I SIMPLE TENSES**

**PRESENT**

| | |
|---|---|
| je me lave | nous nous lavons |
| tu te laves | vous vous lavez |
| il/elle se lave | ils/elles se lavent |

**IMPERFECT**

| | |
|---|---|
| je me lavais | nous nous lavions |
| tu te lavais | vous vous laviez |
| il/elle se lavait | ils/elles se lavaient |

**FUTURE**

| | |
|---|---|
| je me laverai | nous nous laverons |
| tu te laveras | vous vous laverez |
| il/elle se lavera | ils/elles se laveront |

**CONDITIONAL**

| | |
|---|---|
| je me laverais | nous nous laverions |
| tu te laverais | vous vous laveriez |
| il/elle se laverait | ils/elles se laveraient |

**PAST HISTORIC**

| | |
|---|---|
| je me lavai | nous nous lavâmes |
| tu te lavas | vous vous lavâtes |
| il/elle se lava | ils/elles se lavèrent |

**PRESENT SUBJUNCTIVE**

| | |
|---|---|
| je me lave | nous nous lavions |
| tu te laves | vous vous laviez |
| il/elle se lave | ils/elles se lavent |

**IMPERFECT SUBJUNCTIVE**

| | |
|---|---|
| je me lavasse | nous nous lavassions |
| tu te lavasses | vous vous lavassiez |
| il/elle se lavât | ils/elles se lavassent |

---

□ **Reflexive Verbs** (Continued)

Conjugation of: **se laver** to wash (oneself)

II COMPOUND TENSES

PERFECT

| | |
|---|---|
| je me suis lavé(e) | nous nous sommes lavé(e)s |
| tu t'es lavé(e) | vous vous êtes lavé(e)(s) |
| il/elle s'est lavé(e) | ils/elles se sont lavé(e)s |

PLUPERFECT

| | |
|---|---|
| je m'étais lavé(e) | nous nous étions lavé(e)s |
| tu t'étais lavé(e) | vous vous étiez lavé(e)(s) |
| il/elle s'était lavé(e) | ils/elles s'étaient lavé(e)s |

FUTURE PERFECT

| | |
|---|---|
| je me serai lavé(e) | nous nous serons lavé(e)s |
| tu te seras lavé(e) | vous vous serez lavé(e)(s) |
| il/elle se sera lavé(e) | ils/elles se seront lavé(e)s |

CONDITIONAL PERFECT

| | |
|---|---|
| je me serais lavé(e) | nous nous serions lavé(e)s |
| tu te serais lavé(e) | vous vous seriez lavé(e)(s) |
| il/elle se serait lavé(e) | ils/elles se seraient lavé(e)s |

PAST ANTERIOR

| | |
|---|---|
| je me fus lavé(e) | nous nous fûmes lavé(e)s |
| tu te fus lavé(e) | vous vous fûtes lavé(e)(s) |
| il/elle se fut lavé(e) | ils/elles se furent lavé(e)s |

PERFECT SUBJUNCTIVE

| | |
|---|---|
| je me sois lavé(e) | nous nous soyons lavé(e)s |
| tu te sois lavé(e) | vous vous soyez lavé(e)(s) |
| il/elle se soit lavé(e) | ils/elles se soient lavé(e)s |

PLUPERFECT SUBJUNCTIVE

| | |
|---|---|
| je me fusse lavé(e) | nous nous fussions lavé(e)s |
| tu te fusses lavé(e) | vous vous fussiez lavé(e)(s) |
| il/elle se fût lavé(e) | ils/elles se fussent lavé(e)s |

## □ The Passive

In the passive, the subject *receives* the action (e.g. *I was hit*) as opposed to *performing* it (e.g. *I hit him*). In English the verb 'to be' is used with the past participle. In French the passive is formed in exactly the same way, i.e.:

a tense of **être** + past participle.

The past participle agrees in number and gender with the subject → ①

A sample verb is conjugated in the passive voice on pp 38 and 39.

♦ The indirect object in French cannot become the subject in the passive:

in **quelqu'un m'a donné un livre** the indirect object **m'** cannot become the subject of a passive verb (unlike English: *someone gave me a book* → *I was given a book*).

♦ The passive meaning is often expressed in French by:

– **on** plus a verb in the active voice → ②
– a reflexive verb (see p 30) → ③

[1] **Philippe a été récompensé**
Phillip has been rewarded
**Cette peinture est très admirée**
This painting is greatly admired
**Ils le feront pourvu qu'ils soient payés**
They'll do it provided they're paid
**Les enfants seront félicités**
The children will be congratulated
**Cette mesure aurait été critiquée si …**
This measure would have been criticized if …
**Les portes avaient été fermées**
The doors had been closed

[2] **On leur a envoyé une lettre**
They were sent a letter
**On nous a montré le jardin**
We were shown the garden
**On m'a dit que …**
I was told that …

[3] **Ils se vendent 30 francs (la) pièce**
They are sold for 30 francs each
**Ce mot ne s'emploie plus**
This word is no longer used

□ **The Passive** (Continued)

Conjugation of: **être aimé** to *be liked*

PRESENT
je suis aimé(e)
tu es aimé(e)
il/elle est aimé(e)

nous sommes aimé(e)s
vous êtes aimé(e)(s)
ils/elles sont aimé(e)s

IMPERFECT
j'étais aimé(e)
tu étais aimé(e)
il/elle était aimé(e)

nous étions aimé(e)s
vous étiez aimé(e)(s)
ils/elles étaient aimé(e)s

FUTURE
je serai aimé(e)
tu seras aimé(e)
il/elle sera aimé(e)

nous serons aimé(e)s
vous serez aimé(e)(s)
ils/elles seront aimé(e)s

CONDITIONAL
je serais aimé(e)
tu serais aimé(e)
il/elle serait aimé(e)

nous serions aimé(e)s
vous seriez aimé(e)(s)
ils/elles seraient aimé(e)s

PAST HISTORIC
je fus aimé(e)
tu fus aimé(e)
il/elle fut aimé(e)

nous fûmes aimé(e)s
vous fûtes aimé(e)(s)
ils/elles furent aimé(e)s

PRESENT SUBJUNCTIVE
je sois aimé(e)
tu sois aimé(e)
il/elle soit aimé(e)

nous soyons aimé(e)s
vous soyez aimé(e)(s)
ils/elles soient aimé(e)s

IMPERFECT SUBJUNCTIVE
je fusse aimé(e)
tu fusses aimé(e)
il/elle fût aimé(e)

nous fussions aimé(e)s
vous fussiez aimé(e)(s)
ils/elles fussent aimé(e)s

□ **The Passive** (Continued)

Conjugation of: **être aimé** to be liked

---

**PERFECT**

j'ai été aimé(e)
tu as été aimé(e)
il/elle a été aimé(e)

nous avons été aimé(e)s
vous avez été aimé(e)(s)
ils/elles ont été aimé(e)s

**PLUPERFECT**

j'avais été aimé(e)
tu avais été aimé(e)
il/elle avait été aimé(e)

nous avions été aimé(e)s
vous aviez été aimé(e)(s)
ils/elles avaient été aimé(e)s

**FUTURE PERFECT**

j'aurai été aimé(e)
tu auras été aimé(e)
il/elle aura été aimé(e)

nous aurons été aimé(e)s
vous aurez été aimé(e)(s)
ils/elles auront été aimé(e)s

**CONDITIONAL PERFECT**

j'aurais été aimé(e)
tu aurais été aimé(e)
il/elle aurait été aimé(e)

nous aurions été aimé(e)s
vous auriez été aimé(e)(s)
ils/elles auraient été aimé(e)s

**PAST ANTERIOR**

j'eus été aimé(e)
tu eus été aimé(e)
il/elle eut été aimé(e)

nous eûmes été aimé(e)s
vous eûtes été aimé(e)(s)
ils/elles eurent été aimé(e)s

**PERFECT SUBJUNCTIVE**

j'aie été aimé(e)
tu aies été aimé(e)
il/elle ait été aimé(e)

nous ayons été aimé(e)s
vous ayez été aimé(e)(s)
ils/elles aient été aimé(e)s

**PLUPERFECT SUBJUNCTIVE**

j'eusse été aimé(e)
tu eusses été aimé(e)
il/elle eût été aimé(e)

nous eussions été aimé(e)s
vous eussiez été aimé(e)(s)
ils/elles eussent été aimé(e)s

## ◻ Impersonal Verbs

Impersonal verbs are used only in the infinitive and in the third person singular with the subject pronoun **il**, generally translated *it*.

e.g. **il pleut**
*it's raining*
**il est facile de dire que …**
*it's easy to say that …*

The most common impersonal verbs are:

| INFINITIVE | CONSTRUCTIONS |
|---|---|
| **s'agir** | **il s'agit de** + noun → 1 |
| | *it's a question/matter of something,* |
| | *it's about something* |
| | **il s'agit de** + infinitive → 2 |
| | *it's a question/matter of doing; somebody must do* |
| **falloir** | **il faut** + noun object (+ indirect object) → 3 |
| | *(somebody) needs something, something is* |
| | *necessary (to somebody)* |
| | **il faut** + infinitive (+ indirect object) → 4 |
| | *it is necessary to do* |
| | **il faut que** + subjunctive → 5 |
| | *it is necessary to do, somebody must do* |
| **grêler** | **il grêle** |
| | *it's hailing* |
| **neiger** | **il neige** |
| | *it's snowing* → 6 |
| **pleuvoir** | **il pleut** |
| | *it's raining* |
| **tonner** | **il tonne** |
| | *it's thundering* |
| **valoir mieux** | **il vaut mieux** + infinitive → 7 |
| | *it's better to do* |
| | **il vaut mieux que** + subjunctive → 8 |
| | *it's better to do/that somebody does* |

1. **Il ne s'agit pas d'argent**
   It isn't a question/matter of money
   **De quoi s'agit-il?**
   What is it about?
   **Il s'agit de la vie d'une famille au début du siècle**
   It's about the life of a family at the turn of the century

2. **Il s'agit de faire vite**
   We must act quickly

3. **Il faut du courage pour faire ça**
   One needs courage to do that; Courage is needed to do that
   **Il me faut une chaise de plus**
   I need an extra chair

4. **Il faut partir**
   It is necessary to leave; We/I/You must leave*
   **Il me fallait prendre une décision**
   I had to make a decision

5. **Il faut que vous partiez**
   You have to leave/You must leave
   **Il faudrait que je fasse mes valises**
   I should have to/ought to pack my cases

6. **Il pleuvait à verse**
   It was raining heavily/It was pouring

7. **Il vaut mieux refuser**
   It's better to refuse; You/He/I had better refuse*
   **Il vaudrait mieux rester**
   You/We/She had better stay*

8. **Il vaudrait mieux que nous ne venions pas**
   It would be better if we didn't come; We'd better not come

---

\* The translation here obviously depends on context

☐ **Impersonal Verbs** *(Continued)*

The following verbs are also commonly used in impersonal constructions:

| INFINITIVE | CONSTRUCTIONS |
|---|---|
| avoir | **il y a** + noun → 1 <br> *there is/are* |
| être | **il est** + noun → 2 <br> *it is, there are* (very literary style) <br> **il est** + adjective + **de** + infinitive → 3 <br> *it is* |
| faire | **il fait** + adjective of weather → 4 <br> *it is* <br> **il fait** + noun depicting weather/dark/light *etc* <br> *it is* → 5 |
| manquer | **il manque** + noun (+ indirect object) → 6 <br> *there is/are … missing, something is missing/lacking* |
| paraître | **il paraît que** + subjunctive → 7 <br> *it seems/appears that* <br> **il paraît** + indirect object + **que** + indicative → 8 <br> *it seems/appears to somebody that* |
| rester | **il reste** + noun (+ indirect object) → 9 <br> *there is/are … left, (somebody) has something left* |
| sembler | **il semble que** + subjunctive → 10 <br> *it seems/appears that* <br> **il semble** + indirect object + **que** + indicative → 11 <br> *it seems/appears to somebody that* |
| suffire | **il suffit de** + infinitive → 12 <br> *it is enough to do* <br> **il suffit de** + noun → 13 <br> *something is enough, it only takes something* |

1. **Il y a du pain (qui reste)**
   There is some bread (left)
   **Il n'y avait pas de lettres ce matin**
   There were no letters this morning

2. **Il est dix heures**
   It's ten o'clock
   **Il est des gens qui …**
   There are (some) people who …

3. **Il était inutile de protester**
   It was useless to protest
   **Il est facile de critiquer**
   Criticizing is easy

4. **Il fait beau/mauvais**
   It's lovely/horrible weather

5. **Il faisait du soleil/du vent**
   It was sunny/windy
   **Il fait jour/nuit**
   It's light/dark

6. **Il manque deux tasses**
   There are two cups missing; Two cups are missing
   **Il manquait un bouton à sa chemise**
   His shirt had a button missing

7. **Il paraît qu'ils partent demain**
   It appears they are leaving tomorrow

8. **Il nous paraît certain qu'il aura du succès**
   It seems certain to us that he'll be successful

9. **Il reste deux miches de pain**
   There are two loaves left
   **Il lui restait cinquante francs**
   He/She had fifty francs left

10. **Il semble que vous ayez raison**
    It seems that you are right

11. **Il me semblait qu'il conduisait trop vite**
    It seemed to me (that) he was driving too fast

12. **Il suffit de téléphoner pour réserver une place**
    You need only phone to reserve a seat

13. **Il suffit d'une seule erreur pour tout gâcher**
    One single error is enough to ruin everything

## ◻ The Infinitive

The infinitive is the form of the verb found in dictionary entries meaning 'to ... ', e.g. **donner** to give, **vivre** to live.

There are three main types of verbal construction involving the infinitive:

- with no linking preposition → 1
- with the linking preposition **à** → 2 (see also p 64)
- with the linking preposition **de** → 3 (see also p 64)

Verbs followed by an infinitive with no linking preposition

- **devoir, pouvoir, savoir, vouloir** and **falloir** (i.e. modal auxiliary verbs: p 52 → 1).
- **valoir mieux**: see Impersonal Verbs, p 40.
- verbs of seeing or hearing e.g. **voir** to see, **entendre** to hear → 4
- intransitive verbs of motion e.g. **aller** to go, **descendre** to come/go down → 5
- **envoyer** to send → 6
- **faillir** → 7
- **faire** → 8
- **laisser** to let, allow → 9
- The following common verbs:

| | |
|---|---|
| **adorer** | to love |
| **aimer** | to like, love → 10 |
| **aimer mieux** | to prefer → 11 |
| **compter** | to expect |
| **désirer** | to wish, want → 12 |
| **détester** | to hate → 13 |
| **espérer** | to hope → 14 |
| **oser** | to dare → 15 |
| **préférer** | to prefer |
| **sembler** | to seem → 16 |
| **souhaiter** | to wish |

# Examples

*Grammar*

1. **Voulez-vous attendre?**
   Would you like to wait?
2. **J'apprends à nager**
   I'm learning to swim
3. **Essayez de venir**
   Try to come
4. **Il nous a vus arriver**
   He saw us arriving
   **On les entend chanter**
   You can hear them singing
5. **Allez voir Nicolas**
   Go and see Nicholas
   **Descends leur demander**
   Go down and ask them
6. **Je l'ai envoyé les voir**
   I sent him to see them
7. **J'ai failli tomber**
   I almost fell
8. **Ne me faites pas rire!**
   Don't make me laugh!
   **J'ai fait réparer ma valise**
   I've had my case repaired
9. **Laissez-moi passer**
   Let me pass
10. **Il aime nous accompagner**
    He likes to come with us
11. **J'aimerais mieux le choisir moi-même**
    I'd rather choose it myself
12. **Elle ne désire pas venir**
    She doesn't wish to come
13. **Je déteste me lever le matin**
    I hate getting up in the morning
14. **Espérez-vous aller en vacances?**
    Are you hoping to go on holiday?
15. **Nous n'avons pas osé y retourner**
    We haven't dared go back
16. **Vous semblez être inquiet**
    You seem to be worried

## ❏ The Infinitive: Set Expressions

The following are set in French with the meaning shown:

| | | |
|---|---|---|
| **aller chercher** | _to go for, to go and get_ | → ① |
| **envoyer chercher** | _to send for_ | → ② |
| **entendre dire que** | _to hear it said that_ | → ③ |
| **entendre parler de** | _to hear of/about_ | → ④ |
| **faire entrer** | _to show in_ | → ⑤ |
| **faire sortir** | _to let out_ | → ⑥ |
| **faire venir** | _to send for_ | → ⑦ |
| **laisser tomber** | _to drop_ | → ⑧ |
| **vouloir dire** | _to mean_ | → ⑨ |

### The Perfect Infinitive

- The perfect infinitive is formed using the auxiliary verb **avoir** or **être** as appropriate with the past participle of the verb → ⑩

- The perfect infinitive is found:

  – following the preposition **après** _after_ → ⑪
  – following certain verbal constructions → ⑫

1. **Va chercher tes photos**
   Go and get your photos
   **Il est allé chercher Alexandre**
   He's gone to get Alexander

2. **J'ai envoyé chercher un médecin**
   I've sent for a doctor

3. **J'ai entendu dire qu'il est malade**
   I've heard it said that he's ill

4. **Je n'ai plus entendu parler de lui**
   I didn't hear anything more (said) of him

5. **Fais entrer nos invités**
   Show our guests in

6. **J'ai fait sortir le chat**
   I've let the cat out

7. **Je vous ai fait venir parce que …**
   I sent for you because …

8. **Il a laissé tomber le vase**
   He dropped the vase

9. **Qu'est-ce que cela veut dire?**
   What does that mean?

10. | **avoir fini** | **être allé** | **s'être levé** |
    |---|---|---|
    | to have finished | to have gone | to have got up |

11. **Après avoir pris cette décision, il nous a appelé**
    After making/having made that decision, he called us
    **Après être sorties, elles se sont dirigées vers le parking**
    After leaving/having left, they headed for the car park
    **Après nous être levé(e)s, nous avons lu les journaux**
    After getting up/having got up, we read the papers

12. **pardonner à qn d'avoir fait**
    to forgive sb for doing/having done
    **remercier qn d'avoir fait**
    to thank sb for doing/having done
    **regretter d'avoir fait**
    to be sorry for doing/having done

## ❐ The Present Participle

### Formation

- **1st conjugation**
  Replace the **-er** of the infinitive by **-ant** → ①
  - Verbs ending in **-cer**: **c** changes to **ç** → ②
  - Verbs ending in **-ger**: **g** changes to **ge** → ③
- **2nd conjugation**
  Replace the **-ir** of the infinitive by **-issant** → ④
- **3rd conjugation**
  Replace the **-re** of the infinitive by **-ant** → ⑤
- For irregular present participles, see irregular verbs, pp 74 ff.

### Uses

The present participle has a more restricted use in French than in English.

- Used as a verbal form, the present participle is invariable. It is found:
  - on its own, where it corresponds to the English present participle
    → ⑥
  - following the preposition **en** → ⑦

    ⚠ NOTE, in particular, the construction:

      verb + **en** + present participle

      which is often translated by an English phrasal verb, i.e. one
      followed by a preposition like to run down, to bring up → ⑧

- Used as an adjective, the present participle agrees in number and gender with the noun or pronoun → ⑨

  ⚠ NOTE, in particular, the use of **ayant** and **étant** – the present participles of the auxiliary verbs **avoir** and **être** – with a past participle → ⑩

| | | | |
|---|---|---|---|
| **1** | **donner** | → | **donnant** |
| | to give | | giving |
| **2** | **lancer** | → | **lançant** |
| | to throw | | throwing |
| **3** | **manger** | → | **mangeant** |
| | to eat | | eating |
| **4** | **finir** | → | **finissant** |
| | to finish | | finishing |
| **5** | **vendre** | → | **vendant** |
| | to sell | | selling |

**6**    **David, habitant près de Paris, a la possibilité de …**
David, living near Paris, has the opportunity of…
**Elle, pensant que je serais fâché, a dit '…'**
She, thinking that I would be angry, said '…'
**Ils m'ont suivi, criant à tue-tête**
They followed me, shouting at the top of their voices

**7**    **En attendant sa sœur, Richard s'est endormi**
While waiting for his sister, Richard fell asleep
**Téléphone-nous an arrivant chez toi**
Telephone us when you get home
**En appuyant sur ce bouton, on peut …**
By pressing this button, you can …
**Il s'est blessé en essayant de sauver un chat**
He hurt himself trying to rescue a cat

**8**    **sortir en courant**
to run out *(literally: to go out running)*
**avancer en boîtant**
to limp along *(literally: to go forward limping)*

**9**    **le soleil couchant**      **une lumière éblouissante**
the setting sun         a dazzling light
**ils sont déroutants**      **elles étaient étonnantes**
they are disconcerting    they were surprising

**10**    **Ayant mangé plus tôt, il a pu …**
Having eaten earlier, he was able to …
**Étant arrivée en retard, elle a dû …**
Having arrived late, she had to …

## ◻ Past Participle Agreement

Like adjectives, a past participle must sometimes agree in number and gender with a noun or pronoun. For the rules of agreement, see below. Example: **donné**

|        | MASCULINE | FEMININE |
|--------|-----------|----------|
| SING.  | donné     | donnée   |
| PLUR.  | donnés    | données  |

- When the masculine singular form already ends in **-s**, no further **s** is added in the masculine plural, e.g. **pris** *taken*.

### Rules of Agreement in Compound Tenses

- When the auxiliary verb is **avoir**

  The past participle remains in the masculine singular form, unless a direct object precedes the verb. The past participle then agrees in number and gender with the preceding direct object → 1

- When the auxiliary verb is **être**

  The past participle of a non-reflexive verb agrees in number and gender with the subject → 2

  The past participle of a reflexive verb agrees in number and gender with the reflexive pronoun, if the pronoun is a direct object → 3

  No agreement is made if the reflexive pronoun is an indirect object → 4

### The Past Participle as an adjective

The past participle agrees in number and gender with the noun or pronoun → 5

1. **Voici le livre que vous avez demandé**
Here's the book you asked for
**Laquelle avaient-elles choisie?**
Which one had they chosen?
**Ces amis? Je les ai rencontrés à Édimbourg**
Those friends? I met them in Edinburgh
**Il a gardé toutes les lettres qu'elle a écrites**
He has kept all the letters she wrote

2. **Est-ce que ton frère est allé à l'étranger?**
Did your brother go abroad?
**Elle était restée chez elle**
She had stayed at home
**Ils sont partis dans la matinée**
They left in the morning
**Mes cousines sont revenues hier**
My cousins came back yesterday

3. **Tu t'es rappelé d'acheter du pain, Georges?**
Did you remember to buy bread, George?
**Martine s'est demandée pourquoi il l'appelait**
Martine wondered why he was calling her
**'Lui et moi nous nous sommes cachés' a-t-elle dit**
'He and I hid,' she said
**Les vendeuses se sont mises en grève**
Shop assistants have gone on strike
**Vous vous êtes brouillés?**
Have you fallen out with each other?
**Les ouvrières s'étaient entraidées**
The workers had helped one another

4. **Elle s'est lavé les mains**
She washed her hands
**Ils se sont parlé pendant des heures**
They talked to each other for hours

5. **à un moment donné**          **la porte ouverte**
at a given time                  the open door
**ils sont bien connus**         **elles semblent fatiguées**
they are well-known              they seem tired

## ❏ Modal Auxiliary Verbs

- In French, the modal auxiliary verbs are: **devoir**, **pouvoir**, **savoir**, **vouloir** and **falloir**.

- They are followed by a verb in the infinitive and have the following meanings:

| | | |
|---|---|---|
| **devoir** | *to have to, must* → ⬚1 | |
| | *to be due to* → ⬚2 | |
| | in the conditional/conditional perfect: | |
| | *should/should have, ought/ought to have* → ⬚3 | |
| | | |
| **pouvoir** | *to be able to, can* → ⬚4 | |
| | *to be allowed to, can, may* → ⬚5 | |
| | indicating possibility: *may/might/could* → ⬚6 | |
| | | |
| **savoir** | *to know how to, can* → ⬚7 | |
| | | |
| **vouloir** | *to want/wish to* → ⬚8 | |
| | *to be willing to, will* → ⬚9 | |
| | in polite phrases → ⬚10 | |
| | | |
| **falloir** | *to be necessary:* | see Impersonal Verbs, p 40. |

1. **Je dois leur rendre visite**
   I must visit them
   **Elle a dû partir**
   She (has) had to leave
   **Il a dû regretter d'avoir parlé**
   He must have been sorry he spoke

2. **Vous devez revenir demain**
   You're due (to come) back tomorrow
   **Je devais attraper le train de neuf heures mais …**
   I was (supposed) to catch the nine o'clock train but …

3. **Je devrais le faire**
   I ought to do it
   **J'aurais dû m'excuser**
   I ought to have apologized

4. **Il ne peut pas lever le bras**
   He can't raise his arm
   **Pouvez-vous réparer cette montre?**
   Can you mend this watch?

5. **Puis-je les accompagner?**
   May I go with them?

6. **Il peut encore changer d'avis**
   He may change his mind yet
   **Cela pourrait être vrai**
   It could/might be true

7. **Savez-vous conduire?**
   Can you drive?
   **Je ne sais pas faire une omelette**
   I don't know how to make an omelette

8. **Elle veut rester encore un jour**
   She wants to stay another day

9. **Ils ne voulaient pas le faire**
   They wouldn't do it/They weren't willing to do it
   **Ma voiture ne veut pas démarrer**
   My car won't start

10. **Voulez-vous boire quelque chose?**
    Would you like something to drink?

## ◻ Use of Tenses

### The Present

- Unlike English, French does not distinguish between the simple present (e.g. *I smoke, he reads, we live*) and the continuous present (e.g. *I am smoking, he is reading, we are living*) → ①

- To emphasize continuity, the following constructions may be used:

  être en train de faire ⎫
  être à faire ⎭      *to be doing* → ②

- French uses the present tense where English uses the perfect in the following cases:

  – with certain prepositions of time – notably **depuis** *for/since* – when an action begun in the past is continued in the present → ③

  Note, however, that the perfect is used as in English when the verb is negative or the action has been completed → ④

  – in the construction **venir de faire** *to have just done* → ⑤

### The Future

The future is generally used as in English, but note the following:

- Immediate future time is often expressed by means of the present tense of **aller** plus an infinitive → ⑥

- In time clauses expressing future action, French uses the future where English uses the present → ⑦

### The Future Perfect

- Used as in English to mean *shall/will have done* → ⑧

- In time clauses expressing future action, where English uses the perfect tense → ⑨

*grammar*

1. **Je fume**
I smoke OR I am smoking
**Il lit**
He reads OR He is reading
**Nous habitons**
We live OR We are living

2. **Il est en train de travailler**
He's (busy) working

3. **Paul apprend à nager depuis six mois**
Paul's been learning to swim for six months *(and still is)*
**Je suis debout depuis sept heures**
I've been up since seven
**Il y a longtemps que vous attendez?**
Have you been waiting long?
**Voilà deux semaines que nous sommes ici**
That's two weeks we've been here *(now)*

4. **Ils ne se sont pas vus depuis des mois**
They haven't seen each other for months
**Elle est revenue il y a un an**
She came back a year ago

5. **Élisabeth vient de partir**
Elizabeth has just left

6. **Tu vas tomber si tu ne fais pas attention**
You'll fall if you're not careful
**Il va manquer le train**
He's going to miss the train
**Ça va prendre une demi-heure**
It'll take half an hour

7. **Quand il viendra vous serez en vacances**
When he comes you'll be on holiday
**Faites-nous savoir aussitôt qu'elle arrivera**
Let us know as soon as she arrives

8. **J'aurai fini dans une heure**
I shall have finished in an hour

9. **Quand tu auras lu ce roman, rends-le-moi**
When you've read the novel, give it back to me
**Je partirai dès que j'aurai fini**
I'll leave as soon as I've finished

## ❏ Use of Tenses *(Continued)*

### The Imperfect

- The imperfect describes:
  - an action (or state) in the past without definite limits in time → ①
  - habitual action(s) in the past (often translated by means of *would* or *used to*) → ②

- French uses the imperfect tense where English uses the pluperfect in the following cases:
  - with certain prepositions of time – notably **depuis** *for/since* – when an action begun in the remoter past was continued in the more recent past → ③

  Note, however, that the pluperfect *is* used as in English, when the verb is negative or the action has been completed → ④
  - in the construction **venir de faire** *to have just done* → ⑤

### The Perfect

- The perfect is used to recount a completed action or event in the past. Note that this corresponds to a perfect tense or a simple past tense in English → ⑥

### The Past Historic

- Only ever used in *written, literary* French, the past historic recounts a completed action in the past, corresponding to a simple past tense in English → ⑦

### The Past Anterior

This tense is used instead of the pluperfect when a verb in another part of the sentence is in the past historic. That is

- in time clauses, after conjunctions like: **quand**, **lorsque** *when*, **dès que**, **aussitôt que** *as soon as*, **après que** *after* → ⑧
- after **à peine** *hardly, scarcely* → ⑨

### The Subjunctive

- In spoken French, the present subjunctive generally replaces the imperfect subjunctive. See also pp 58 ff.

1    **Elle regardait par la fenêtre**
She was looking out of the window
**Il pleuvait quand je suis sorti de chez moi**
It was raining when I left the house
**Nos chambres donnaient sur la plage**
Our rooms overlooked the beach

2    **Dans sa jeunesse, il se levait à l'aube**
In his youth he got up at dawn
**Nous causions des heures entières**
We would talk for hours on end
**Elle te taquinait, n'est-ce pas?**
She used to tease you, didn't she?

3    **Nous habitions à Londres depuis deux ans**
We had been living in London for two years *(and still were)*
**Il était malade depuis 1985**
He had been ill since 1985
**Il y avait assez longtemps qu'il le faisait**
He had been doing it for quite a long time

4    **Voilà un an que je ne l'avais pas vu**
I hadn't seen him for a year
**Il y avait une heure qu'elle était arrivée**
She had arrived one hour before

5    **Je venais de les rencontrer**
I had just met them

6    **Nous sommes allés au bord de la mer**
We went/have been to the seaside
**Il a refusé de nous aider**
He (has) refused to help us
**La voiture ne s'est pas arrêtée**
The car didn't stop/hasn't stopped

7    **Le roi mourut en 1592**
The king died in 1592

8    **Quand il eut fini, il se leva**
When he had finished, he got up

9    **À peine eut-il parlé qu'on frappa à la porte**
He had scarcely spoken when there was a knock at the door

## ❏ The Subjunctive: when to use it

**(For how to form the subjunctive see pp 6 ff.)**

* After certain conjunctions

| | |
|---|---|
| quoique ⎱ bien que ⎰ | *although* → ① |
| pour que ⎱ afin que ⎰ | *so that* → ② |
| pourvu que | *provided that* → ③ |
| jusqu'à ce que | *until* → ④ |
| avant que (... ne) | *before* → ⑤ |
| à moins que (... ne) | *unless* → ⑥ |
| de peur que (... ne) ⎱ de crainte que (... ne) ⎰ | *for fear that, lest* → ⑦ |

⚠ NOTE that the **ne** following the conjunctions in examples ⑤ to ⑦ has no translation value. It is often omitted in spoken informal French.

* After the conjunctions

| | |
|---|---|
| de sorte que ⎱ de façon que ⎬ de manière que ⎰ | *so that* (indicating a *purpose*) → ⑧ |

When these conjunctions introduce a *result* and not a *purpose*, the subjunctive is not used → ⑨

* After impersonal constructions which express necessity, possibility etc

| | |
|---|---|
| il faut que ⎱ il est nécessaire que ⎰ | *it is necessary that* → ⑩ |
| il est possible que | *it is possible that* → ⑪ |
| il semble que | *it seems that* → ⑫ |
| il vaut mieux que | *it is better that* → ⑬ |
| il est dommage que | *it's a pity that* → ⑭ |

# Examples

1. **Bien qu'il fasse beaucoup d'efforts, il est peu récompensé**
   Although he makes a lot of effort, he isn't rewarded for it

2. **Demandez un reçu afin que vous puissiez être remboursé**
   Ask for a receipt so that you can get a refund

3. **Nous partirons ensemble pourvu que Sylvie soit d'accord**
   We'll leave together provided Sylvie agrees

4. **Reste ici jusqu'à ce que nous revenions**
   Stay here until we come back

5. **Je le ferai avant que tu ne partes**
   I'll do it before you leave

6. **Ce doit être Paul, à moins que je ne me trompe**
   That must be Paul, unless I'm mistaken

7. **Parlez bas de peur qu'on ne vous entende**
   Speak softly lest anyone hears you

8. **Retournez-vous de sorte que je vous voie**
   Turn round so that I can see you

9. **Il refuse de le faire de sorte que je dois le faire moi-même**
   He refuses to do it so that I have to do it myself

10. **Il faut que je vous parle immédiatement**
    I must speak to you right away/It is necessary that I speak …

11. **Il est possible qu'ils aient raison**
    They may be right/It's possible that they are right

12. **Il semble qu'elle ne soit pas venue**
    It appears that she hasn't come

13. **Il vaut mieux que vous restiez chez vous**
    It's better that you stay at home

14. **Il est dommage qu'elle ait perdu cette adresse**
    It's a shame/a pity that she's lost the address

☐ **The Subjunctive: when to use it** *(Continued)*

- After verbs of:
  - 'wishing'

    **vouloir que**
    **désirer que**      *to wish that, want* → 1
    **souhaiter que**

  - 'fearing'

    **craindre que**      *to be afraid that* → 2
    **avoir peur que**

    ⚠ NOTE that **ne** in the first phrase of example 2 has no translation value. It is often omitted in spoken informal French.

  - 'ordering', 'forbidding', 'allowing'

    **ordonner que**     *to order that* → 3
    **défendre que**     *to forbid that* → 4
    **permettre que**    *to allow that* → 5

  - opinion, expressing uncertainty

    **croire que**
    **penser que**     *to think that* → 6
    **douter que**      *to doubt that* → 7

  - emotion (e.g. regret, shame, pleasure)

    **regretter que** *to be sorry that* → 8
    **être content/surpris** *etc* **que** *to be pleased/surprised etc that* → 9

- After a superlative → 10

- After certain adjectives expressing some sort of 'uniqueness'

    **dernier ... qui/que**     *last ... who/that*
    **premier ... qui/que**    *first ... who/that*
    **meilleur ... qui/que**   *best ... who/that*      → 11
    **seul**
    **unique** **... qui/que**     *only ... who/that*

# Examples

1. **Nous voulons qu'elle soit contente**
   We want her to be happy *(literally: We want that she is happy)*
   **Désirez-vous que je le fasse?**
   Do you want me to do it?

2. **Il craint qu'il ne soit trop tard**
   He's afraid it may be too late
   **Avez-vous peur qu'il ne revienne pas?**
   Are you afraid that he won't come back?

3. **Il a ordonné qu'ils soient désormais à l'heure**
   He has ordered that they be on time from now on

4. **Elle défend que vous disiez cela**
   She forbids you to say that

5. **Permettez que nous vous aidions**
   Allow us to help you

6. **Je ne pense pas qu'ils soient venus**
   I don't think they came

7. **Nous doutons qu'il ait dit la vérité**
   We doubt that he told the truth

8. **Je regrette que vous ne puissiez pas venir**
   I'm sorry that you cannot come

9. **Je suis content que vous les aimiez**
   I'm pleased that you like them

10. **la personne la plus sympathique que je connaisse**
    the nicest person I know
    **l'article le moins cher que j'aie jamais acheté**
    the cheapest item I have ever bought

11. **Voici la dernière lettre qu'elle m'ait écrite**
    This is the last letter she wrote to me
    **David est la seule personne qui puisse me conseiller**
    David is the only person who can advise me

## ☐ The Subjunctive: when to use it *(Continued)*

- After      **si ( ... ) que**    *however*    → 1
                 **qui que**      *whoever*    → 2
                 **quoi que**    *whatever*    → 3

- After **que** in the following:
  - to form the 3rd person imperative or to express a wish → 4
  - when **que** has the meaning *if*, replacing **si** in a clause → 5
  - when **que** has the meaning *whether* → 6

- In relative clauses following certain types of indefinite and negative construction → 7/8

- In set expressions → 9

1. **si courageux qu'il soit**
   however brave he may be
   **si peu que ce soit**
   however little it is

2. **Qui que vous soyez, allez-vous-en!**
   Whoever you are, go away!

3. **Quoi que nous fassions, ...**
   Whatever we do, ...

4. **Qu'il entre!**
   Let him come in!
   **Que cela vous serve de leçon!**
   Let that be a lesson to you!

5. **S'il fait beau et que tu te sentes mieux, nous irons ...**
   If it's nice and you're feeling better, we'll go ...

6. **Que tu viennes ou non, je ...**
   Whether you come or not, I ...

7. **Il cherche une maison qui ait deux caves**
   He's looking for a house which has two cellars
   *(subjunctive used since such a house may or may not exist)*
   **J'ai besoin d'un livre qui décrive l'art du mime**
   I need a book which describes the art of mime
   *(subjunctive used since such a book may or may not exist)*

8. **Je n'ai rencontré personne qui la connaisse**
   I haven't met anyone who knows her
   **Il n'y a rien qui puisse vous empêcher de ...**
   There's nothing that can prevent you from ...

9. **Vive le roi!**
   Long live the king!
   **Que Dieu vous bénisse!**
   God bless you!

## ❑ Verbs governing à and de

The following lists (pp 64 to 72) contain common verbal constructions using the prepositions **à** and **de**

Note the following abbreviations:

| infin. | infinitive | **qn** | quelqu'un |
| perf. infin. | perfect infinitive* | *sb* | somebody |
| **qch** | quelque chose | *sth* | something |

*For formation see p 46

| | |
|---|---|
| **accuser qn de qch/de** + perf. infin. | to accuse sb of sth/of doing, having done → ① |
| **accoutumer qn à qch/à** + infin. | to accustom sb to sth/to doing |
| **acheter qch à qn** | to buy sth from sb/for sb → ② |
| **achever de** + infin. | to end up doing |
| **aider qn à** + infin. | to help sb to do → ③ |
| **s'amuser à** + infin. | to have fun doing |
| **s'apercevoir de qch** | to notice sth → ④ |
| **apprendre qch à qn** | to teach sb sth |
| **apprendre à** + infin. | to learn to do → ⑤ |
| **apprendre à qn à** + infin. | to teach sb to do → ⑥ |
| **s'approcher de qn/qch** | to approach sb/sth → ⑦ |
| **arracher qch à qn** | to snatch sth from sb → ⑧ |
| **(s')arrêter de** + infin. | to stop doing → ⑨ |
| **arriver à** + infin. | to manage to do → ⑩ |
| **assister à qch** | to attend sth, be at sth |
| **s'attendre à** + infin. | to expect to do → ⑪ |
| **blâmer qn de qch/de** + perf. infin. | to blame sb for sth/for having done → ⑫ |
| **cacher qch à qn** | to hide sth from sb → ⑬ |
| **cesser de** + infin. | to stop doing → ⑭ |

1. **Il m'a accusé d'avoir menti**
   He accused me of lying

2. **Marie-Christine leur a acheté deux billets**
   Marie-Christine bought two tickets from/for them

3. **Aidez-moi à porter ces valises**
   Help me to carry these cases

4. **Il ne s'est pas aperçu de son erreur**
   He didn't notice his mistake

5. **Elle apprend à lire**
   She's learning to read

6. **Je lui apprends à nager**
   I'm teaching him/her to swim

7. **Elle s'est approchée de moi, en disant '...'**
   She came up to me, saying '...'

8. **Le voleur lui a arraché l'argent**
   The thief snatched the money from him/her

9. **Arrêtez de faire du bruit!**
   Stop being (so) noisy!

10. **Je n'arrive pas à le comprendre**
    I can't understand it

11. **Est-ce qu'elle s'attendait à le voir?**
    Was she expecting to see him?

12. **Je ne la blâme pas de l'avoir fait**
    I don't blame her for doing it

13. **Cache-les-leur!**
    Hide them from them!

14. **Est-ce qu'il a cessé de pleuvoir?**
    Has it stopped raining?

## ❑ Verbs governing à and de *(Continued)*

| | |
|---|---|
| **changer de** qch | *to change sth* → [1] |
| **se charger de** qch/de + infin. | *to see to sth/undertake to do* |
| **chercher à** + infin. | *to try to do* |
| **commander à** qn de + infin. | *to order sb to do* → [2] |
| **commencer à/de** + infin. | *to begin to do* → [3] |
| **conseiller à** qn de + infin. | *to advise sb to do* → [4] |
| **consentir à** qch/à + infin. | *to agree to sth/to do* → [5] |
| **continuer à/de** + infin. | *to continue to do* |
| **craindre de** + infin. | *to be afraid to do/of doing* |
| **décider de** + infin. | *to decide to do* → [6] |
| **se décider à** + infin. | *to make up one's mind to do* |
| **défendre à** qn de + infin. | *to forbid sb to do* → [7] |
| **demander** qch **à** qn | *to ask sb sth/for sth* → [8] |
| **demander à** qn de + infin. | *to ask sb to do* → [9] |
| **se dépêcher de** + infin. | *to hurry to do* |
| **dépendre de** qn/qch | *to depend on sb/sth* |
| **déplaire à** qn | *to displease sb* → [10] |
| **désobéir à** qn | *to disobey sb* → [11] |
| **dire à** qn de + infin. | *to tell sb to do* → [12] |
| **dissuader** qn **de** + infin. | *to dissuade sb from doing* |
| **douter de** qch | *to doubt sth* |
| **se douter de** qch | *to suspect sth* |
| **s'efforcer de** + infin. | *to strive to do* |
| **empêcher** qn **de** + infin. | *to prevent sb from doing* → [13] |
| **emprunter** qch **à** qn | *to borrow sth from sb* → [14] |
| **encourager** qn **à** + infin. | *to encourage sb to do* → [15] |
| **enlever** qch **à** qn | *to take sth away from sb* |
| **enseigner** qch **à** qn | *to teach sb sth* |
| **enseigner à** qn **à** + infin. | *to teach sb to do* |
| **entreprendre de** + infin. | *to undertake to do* |
| **essayer de** + infin. | *to try to do* → [16] |
| **eviter de** + infin. | *to avoid doing* → [17] |

1. **J'ai changé d'avis/de robe**
   I changed my mind/my dress
   **Il faut changer de train à Toulouse**
   You have to change trains at Toulouse

2. **Il leur a commandé de tirer**
   He ordered them to shoot

3. **Il commence à neiger**
   It's starting to snow

4. **Il leur a conseillé d'attendre**
   He advised them to wait

5. **Je n'ai pas consenti à l'aider**
   I haven't agreed to help him/her

6. **Qu'est-ce que vous avez décidé de faire?**
   What have you decided to do?

7. **Je leur ai défendu de sortir**
   I've forbidden them to go out

8. **Je lui ai demandé l'heure**
   I asked him/her the time
   **Il lui a demandé un livre**
   He asked him/her for a book

9. **Demande à Alain de le faire**
   Ask Alan to do it

10. **Leur attitude lui déplaît**
    He/She doesn't like their attitude

11. **Ils lui désobéissent souvent**
    They often disobey him/her

12. **Dites-leur de se taire**
    Tell them to be quiet

13. **Le bruit m'empêche de travailler**
    The noise is preventing me from working

14. **Puis-je vous emprunter ce stylo?**
    May I borrow this pen from you?

15. **Elle encourage ses enfants à être indépendants**
    She encourages her children to be independent

16. **Essayez d'arriver à l'heure**
    Try to arrive on time

17. **Il évite de lui parler**
    He avoids speaking to him/her

## ❐ Verbs governing à and de (Continued)

| | |
|---|---|
| **s'excuser de qch/de** + (perf.) infin. | to apologize for sth/for doing, having done → 1 |
| **exceller à** + infin. | to excel at doing |
| **se fâcher de qch** | to be annoyed at sth |
| **feindre de** + infin. | to pretend to do → 2 |
| **féliciter qn de qch/de** + (perf.) infin. | to congratulate sb on sth/on doing, having done → 3 |
| **se fier à qn** | to trust sb → 4 |
| **finir de** + infin. | to finish doing → 5 |
| **forcer qn à** + infin. | to force sb to do |
| **habituer qn à** + infin. | to accustom sb to doing |
| **s'habituer à** + infin. | to get/be used to doing → 6 |
| **se hâter de** + infin. | to hurry to do |
| **hésiter à** + infin. | to hesitate to do |
| **interdire à qn de** + infin. | to forbid sb to do → 7 |
| **s'intéresser à qn/qch/à** + infin. | to be interested in sb/sth/in doing → 8 |
| **inviter qn à** + infin. | to invite sb to do → 9 |
| **jouer à** (+ sports, games) | to play → 10 |
| **jouer de** (+ musical instruments) | to play → 11 |
| **jouir de qch** | to enjoy sth → 12 |
| **jurer de** + infin. | to swear to do |
| **louer qn de qch** | to praise sb for sth |
| **manquer à qn** | to be missed by sb → 13 |
| **manquer de qch** | to lack sth |
| **manquer de** + infin. | to fail to do → 14 |
| **se marier à qn** | to marry sb |
| **se méfier de qn** | to distrust sb |
| **menacer de** + infin. | to threaten to do → 15 |
| **mériter de** + infin. | to deserve to do → 16 |
| **se mettre à** + infin. | to begin to do |
| **se moquer de qn/qch** | to make fun of sb/sth |
| **négliger de** + infin. | to fail to do |

1. **Je m'excuse d'être (arrivé) en retard**
   I apologize for being/arriving late

2. **Elle feint de dormir**
   She's pretending to be asleep

3. **Je l'ai félicitée d'avoir gagné**
   I congratulated her on winning

4. **Je ne me fie pas à ces gens-là**
   I don't trust those people

5. **Avez-vous fini de lire ce journal?**
   Have you finished reading this newspaper?

6. **Il s'est habitué à boire moins de café**
   He got used to drinking less coffee

7. **Il a interdit aux enfants de jouer avec des allumettes**
   He's forbidden the children to play with matches

8. **Elle s'intéresse beaucoup au sport**
   She's very interested in sport

9. **Il m'a invitée à danser**
   He asked me to dance

10. **Elle joue au tennis et au hockey**
    She plays tennis and hockey

11. **Il joue du piano et de la guitare**
    He plays the piano and the guitar

12. **Il jouit d'une santé solide**
    He enjoys good health

13. **Tu manques à tes parents**
    Your parents miss you

14. **Je ne manquerai pas de le lui dire**
    I'll be sure to tell him/her about it

15. **Elle a menacé de démissionner tout de suite**
    She threatened to resign at once

16. **Ils méritent d'être promus**
    They deserve to be promoted

## ❒ **Verbs governing à and de** *(Continued)*

| | |
|---|---|
| **nuire à qch** | *to harm sth* → [1] |
| **obéir à qn** | *to obey sb* |
| **obliger qn à** + infin. | *to oblige sb to do* → [2] |
| **s'occuper de qch/qn** | *to look after sth/sb* → [3] |
| **offrir de** + infin. | *to offer to do* → [4] |
| **omettre de** + infin. | *to fail to do* |
| **ordonner à qn de** + infin. | *to order sb to do* → [5] |
| **ôter qch à qn** | *to take sth away from sb* |
| **oublier de** + infin. | *to forget to do* |
| **pardonner qch à qn** | *to forgive sb for sth* |
| **pardonner à qn de** + perf. infin. | *to forgive sb for having done* → [6] |
| **parvenir à** + infin. | *to manage to do* |
| **se passer de qch** | *to do/go without sth* → [7] |
| **penser à qn/qch** | *to think about sb/sth* → [8] |
| **permettre qch à qn** | *to allow sb sth* |
| **permettre à qn de** + infin. | *to allow sb to do* → [9] |
| **persister à** + infin. | *to persist in doing* |
| **persuader qn de** + infin. | *to persuade sb to do* → [10] |
| **se plaindre de qch** | *to complain about sth* |
| **plaire à qn** | *to please sb* → [11] |
| **pousser qn à** + infin. | *to urge sb to do* |
| **prendre qch à qn** | *to take sth from sb* → [12] |
| **préparer qn à** + infin. | *to prepare sb to do* |
| **se préparer à** + infin. | *to get ready to do* |
| **prier qn de** + infin. | *to beg sb to do* |
| **profiter de qch/de** + infin. | *to take advantage of sth/of doing* |
| **promettre à qn de** + infin. | *to promise sb to do* → [13] |
| **proposer de** + infin. | *to suggest doing* → [14] |
| **punir qn de qch** | *to punish sb for sth* → [15] |
| **récompenser qn de qch** | *to reward sb for sth* |
| **réfléchir à qch** | *to think about sth* |
| **refuser de** + infin. | *to refuse to do* → [16] |

| | | |
|---|---|---|
| 1 | **Ce mode de vie va nuire à sa santé** <br> This lifestyle will damage her health | |
| 2 | **Il les a obligés à faire la vaisselle** <br> He made them do the washing-up | |
| 3 | **Je m'occupe de ma nièce** <br> I'm looking after my niece | |
| 4 | **Stuart a offert de nous accompagner** <br> Stuart has offered to go with us | |
| 5 | **Les soldats leur ont ordonné de se rendre** <br> The soldiers ordered them to give themselves up | |
| 6 | **Est-ce que tu as pardonné à Charles de t'avoir menti?** <br> Have you forgiven Charles for lying to you? | |
| 7 | **Nous nous sommes passés d'électricité pendant plusieurs jours** <br> We did without electricity for several days | |
| 8 | **Je pense souvent à toi** <br> I often think about you | |
| 9 | **Permettez-moi de continuer, s'il vous plaît** <br> Allow me to go on, please | |
| 10 | **Elle nous a persuadés de rester** <br> She persuaded us to stay | |
| 11 | **Est-ce que ce genre de film lui plaît?** <br> Does he/she like this kind of film? | |
| 12 | **Je lui ai pris son baladeur** <br> I took his personal stereo from him | |
| 13 | **Ils ont promis à Pascale de venir** <br> They promised Pascale that they would come | |
| 14 | **J'ai proposé de les inviter** <br> I suggested inviting them | |
| 15 | **Il a été puni de sa malhonnêteté** <br> He has been punished for his dishonesty | |
| 16 | **Il a refusé de coopérer** <br> He has refused to cooperate | |

## ☐ Verbs governing à and de (Continued)

| | |
|---|---|
| **regretter de** + perf. infin. | to regret doing, having done → 1 |
| **remercier qn de qch/de** + perf. infin. | to thank sb for sth/for doing, having done → 2 |
| **renoncer à qch/à** + infin. | to give sth up/give up doing |
| **reprocher qch à qn** | to reproach sb with/for sth → 3 |
| **résister à qch** | to resist sth → 4 |
| **résoudre de** + infin. | to resolve to do |
| **ressembler à qn/qch** | to look/be like sb/sth → 5 |
| **réussir à** + infin. | to manage to do → 6 |
| **rire de qn/qch** | to laugh at sb/sth |
| **risquer de** + infin. | to risk doing → 7 |
| **servir à qch/à** + infin. | to be used for sth/for doing → 8 |
| **se servir de qch** | to use sth; to help oneself to sth → 9 |
| **songer à** + infin. | to think of doing |
| **se souvenir de qn/qch/de** + perf. infin. | to remember sb/sth/doing, having done → 10 |
| **succéder à qn** | to succeed sb |
| **survivre à qn** | to outlive sb → 11 |
| **tâcher de** + infin. | to try to do → 12 |
| **tarder à** + infin. | to delay doing → 13 |
| **tendre à** + infin. | to tend to do |
| **tenir à** + infin. | to be keen to do → 14 |
| **tenter de** + infin. | to try to do → 15 |
| **se tromper de qch** | to be wrong about sth → 16 |
| **venir de\*** + infin. | to have just done → 17 |
| **vivre de qch** | to live on sth |
| **voler qch à qn** | to steal sth from sb |

*See also Use of Tenses, pp 54 and 56

| 1 | **Je regrette de ne pas vous avoir écrit plus tôt**<br>I'm sorry for not writing to you sooner |
| 2 | **Nous les avons remerciés de leur gentillesse**<br>We thanked them for their kindness |
| 3 | **On lui reproche son manque d'enthousiasme**<br>They're reproaching him for his lack of enthusiasm |
| 4 | **Comment résistez-vous à la tentation?**<br>How do you resist temptation? |
| 5 | **Elles ressemblent beaucoup à leur mère**<br>They look very like their mother |
| 6 | **Vous avez réussi à me convaincre**<br>You've managed to convince me |
| 7 | **Vous risquez de tomber en faisant cela**<br>You risk falling doing that |
| 8 | **Ce bouton sert à régler le volume**<br>This knob is (used) for adjusting the volume |
| 9 | **Il s'est servi d'un tournevis pour l'ouvrir**<br>He used a screwdriver to open it |
| 10 | **Vous vous souvenez de Lucienne?**<br>Do you remember Lucienne?<br>**Il ne se souvient pas de l'avoir perdu**<br>He doesn't remember losing it |
| 11 | **Elle a survécu à son mari**<br>She outlived her husband |
| 12 | **Tâchez de ne pas être en retard!**<br>Try not to be late! |
| 13 | **Il n'a pas tardé à prendre une décision**<br>He was not long in taking a decision |
| 14 | **Elle tient à le faire elle-même**<br>She's keen to do it herself |
| 15 | **J'ai tenté de la comprendre**<br>I've tried to understand her |
| 16 | **Je me suis trompé de route**<br>I took the wrong road |
| 17 | **Mon père vient de téléphoner**<br>My father's just phoned     **Nous venions d'arriver**<br>We had just arrived |

## ▢ Irregular Verbs

The verbs listed opposite and conjugated on pp 76 to 131 provide the main patterns for irregular verbs. The verbs are grouped opposite according to their infinitive ending (except **avoir** and **être**), and are shown in the following tables in alphabetical order.

In the tables, the most important irregular verbs are given in their most common simple tenses, together with the imperative and the present participle.

The auxiliary (**avoir** or **être**) is also shown for each verb, together with the past participle, to enable you to form all the compound tenses, as on pp 24 and 26.

• For a fuller list of irregular verbs, the reader is referred to Collins Gem French Verb Tables, which shows you how to conjugate some 2000 French verbs.

avoir
être

'-er': aller
envoyer

'-ir': acquérir
bouillir
courir
cueillir
dormir
fuir
haïr
mourir
ouvrir
partir
sentir
servir
sortir
tenir
venir
vêtir

'-oir': s'asseoir
devoir
falloir
pleuvoir
pouvoir
recevoir
savoir
valoir
voir
vouloir

'-re': battre
boire
connaître
coudre
craindre
croire
croître
cuire
dire
écrire
faire
lire
mettre
moudre
naître
paraître
plaire
prendre
résoudre
rire
rompre
suffire
suivre
se taire
vaincre
vivre

| **acquérir** to acquire | Auxiliary: **avoir** |
|---|---|

PAST PARTICIPLE

acquis

PRESENT PARTICIPLE

acquérant

IMPERATIVE

acquiers
acquérons
acquérez

| PRESENT | | IMPERFECT | |
|---|---|---|---|
| | j'acquiers | | j'acquérais |
| tu | acquiers | tu | acquérais |
| il | acquiert | il | acquérait |
| nous | acquérons | nous | acquérions |
| vous | acquérez | vous | acquériez |
| ils | acquierent | ils | acquéraient |

| FUTURE | | CONDITIONAL | |
|---|---|---|---|
| | j'acquerrai | | j'acquerrais |
| tu | acquerras | tu | acquerrais |
| il | acquerra | il | acquerrait |
| nous | acquerrons | nous | acquerrions |
| vous | acquerrez | vous | acquerriez |
| ils | acquerront | ils | acquerraient |

| PRESENT SUBJUNCTIVE | | PAST HISTORIC | |
|---|---|---|---|
| | j'acquière | | j'acquis |
| tu | acquières | tu | acquis |
| il | acquière | il | acquit |
| nous | acquérions | nous | acquîmes |
| vous | acquériez | vous | acquîtes |
| ils | acquièrent | ils | acquirent |

| **aller** *to go* | Auxiliary: **être** |
|---|---|

| PAST PARTICIPLE | IMPERATIVE |
|---|---|
| allé | **va**<br>allons<br>allez |
| PRESENT PARTICIPLE | |
| allant | |

| PRESENT | | IMPERFECT | |
|---|---|---|---|
| **je** | **vais** | | j'allais |
| **tu** | **vas** | tu | allais |
| **il** | **va** | il | allait |
| nous | allons | nous | allions |
| vous | allez | vous | alliez |
| **ils** | **vont** | ils | allaient |

| FUTURE | | CONDITIONAL | |
|---|---|---|---|
| | j'irai | | j'irais |
| **tu** | **iras** | **tu** | **irais** |
| **il** | **ira** | **il** | **irait** |
| **nous** | **irons** | **nous** | **irions** |
| **vous** | **irez** | **vous** | **iriez** |
| **ils** | **iront** | **ils** | **iraient** |

| PRESENT SUBJUNCTIVE | | PAST HISTORIC | |
|---|---|---|---|
| | j'aille | | j'allai |
| **tu** | **ailles** | tu | allas |
| **il** | **aille** | il | alla |
| nous | allions | nous | allâmes |
| vous | alliez | vous | allâtes |
| **ils** | **aillent** | ils | allèrent |

| **s'asseoir** *to sit down* | Auxiliary: **être** |
|---|---|

| PAST PARTICIPLE | IMPERATIVE |
|---|---|
| **assis** | **assieds-toi** |
| | **asseyons-nous** |
| PRESENT PARTICIPLE | **asseyez-vous** |
| **s'asseyant** | |

| PRESENT | IMPERFECT |
|---|---|
| je m'assieds *or* assois | je m'asseyais |
| tu t'assieds *or* assois | tu t'asseyais |
| il s'assied *or* assoit | il s'asseyait |
| nous nous asseyons *or* assoyons | nous nous asseyions |
| vous vous asseyez *or* assoyez | vous vous asseyiez |
| ils s'asseyent *or* assoient | ils s'asseyaient |

| FUTURE | CONDITIONAL |
|---|---|
| je m'assiérai | je m'assiérais |
| tu t'assiéras | tu t'assiérais |
| il s'assiéra | il s'assiérait |
| nous nous assiérons | nous nous assiérions |
| vous vous assiérez | vous vous assiériez |
| ils s'assiéront | ils s'assiéraient |

| PRESENT SUBJUNCTIVE | PAST HISTORIC |
|---|---|
| je m'asseye | je m'assis |
| tu t'asseyes | tu t'assis |
| il s'asseye | il s'assit |
| nous nous asseyions | nous nous assîmes |
| vous vous asseyiez | vous vous assîtes |
| ils s'asseyent | ils s'assirent |

| **avoir** *to have* | Auxiliary: **avoir** |
|---|---|

PAST PARTICIPLE

eu

PRESENT PARTICIPLE

ayant

IMPERATIVE

aie
ayons
ayez

| PRESENT | IMPERFECT |
|---|---|
| j'ai | j'avais |
| tu as | tu avais |
| il a | il avait |
| nous avons | nous avions |
| vous avez | vous aviez |
| ils ont | ils avaient |
| **FUTURE** | **CONDITIONAL** |
| j'aurai | j'aurais |
| tu auras | tu aurais |
| il aura | il aurait |
| nous aurons | nous aurions |
| vous aurez | vous auriez |
| ils auront | ils auraient |
| **PRESENT SUBJUNCTIVE** | **PAST HISTORIC** |
| j'aie | j'eus |
| tu aies | tu eus |
| il ait | il eut |
| nous ayons | nous eûmes |
| vous ayez | vous eûtes |
| ils aient | ils eurent |

| **battre** to beat | Auxiliary: **avoir** |
|---|---|

PAST PARTICIPLE

battu

PRESENT PARTICIPLE

battant

IMPERATIVE

**bats**
battons
battez

| PRESENT | IMPERFECT |
|---|---|
| je **bats** | je battais |
| tu **bats** | tu battais |
| il **bat** | il battait |
| nous battons | nous battions |
| vous battez | vous battiez |
| ils battent | ils battaient |

| FUTURE | CONDITIONAL |
|---|---|
| je battrai | je battrais |
| tu battras | tu battrais |
| il battra | il battrait |
| nous battrons | nous battrions |
| vous battrez | vous battriez |
| ils battront | ils battraient |

| PRESENT SUBJUNCTIVE | PAST HISTORIC |
|---|---|
| je batte | je battis |
| tu battes | tu battis |
| il batte | il battit |
| nous battions | nous battîmes |
| vous battiez | vous battîtes |
| ils battent | ils battirent |

| **boire** _to drink_ | Auxiliary: **avoir** |
|---|---|

| PAST PARTICIPLE | IMPERATIVE |
|---|---|
| **bu** | bois |
| | **buvons** |
| PRESENT PARTICIPLE | **buvez** |
| **buvant** | |

| PRESENT | IMPERFECT |
|---|---|
| je bois | **je buvais** |
| tu bois | **tu buvais** |
| il boit | **il buvait** |
| **nous buvons** | **nous buvions** |
| **vous buvez** | **vous buviez** |
| **ils boivent** | **ils buvaient** |

| FUTURE | CONDITIONAL |
|---|---|
| je boirai | je boirais |
| tu boiras | tu boirais |
| il boira | il boirait |
| nous boirons | nous boirions |
| vous boirez | vous boiriez |
| ils boiront | ils boiraient |

| PRESENT SUBJUNCTIVE | PAST HISTORIC |
|---|---|
| **je boive** | **je bus** |
| **tu boives** | **tu bus** |
| **il boive** | **il but** |
| **nous buvions** | **nous bûmes** |
| **vous buviez** | **vous bûtes** |
| **ils boivent** | **ils burent** |

| **bouillir** *to boil* | Auxiliary: **avoir** |
|---|---|

PAST PARTICIPLE                               IMPERATIVE

bouilli

                                                 **bous**
                                          **bouillons**
PRESENT PARTICIPLE                        **bouillez**

**bouillant**

| PRESENT | IMPERFECT |
|---|---|
| je **bous** | je **bouillais** |
| tu **bous** | tu **bouillais** |
| il **bout** | il **bouillait** |
| nous **bouillons** | nous **bouillions** |
| vous **bouillez** | vous **bouilliez** |
| ils **bouillent** | ils **bouillaient** |

| FUTURE | CONDITIONAL |
|---|---|
| je bouillirai | je bouillirais |
| tu bouilliras | tu bouillirais |
| il bouillira | il bouillirait |
| nous bouillirons | nous bouillirions |
| vous bouillirez | vous bouilliriez |
| ils bouilliront | ils bouilliraient |

| PRESENT SUBJUNCTIVE | PAST HISTORIC |
|---|---|
| je **bouille** | je bouillis |
| tu **bouilles** | tu bouillis |
| il **bouille** | il bouillit |
| nous **bouillions** | nous bouillîmes |
| vous **bouilliez** | vous bouillîtes |
| ils **bouillent** | ils bouillirent |

# VERBS: IRREGULAR

| **connaître** to know | Auxiliary: **avoir** |
|---|---|

PAST PARTICIPLE

**connu**

PRESENT PARTICIPLE

**connaissant**

IMPERATIVE

**connais**
**connaissons**
**connaissez**

| PRESENT | IMPERFECT |
|---|---|
| je **connais** | je **connaissais** |
| tu **connais** | tu **connaissais** |
| il **connaît** | il **connaissait** |
| nous **connaissons** | nous **connaissions** |
| vous **connaissez** | vous **connaissiez** |
| ils **connaissent** | ils **connaissaient** |

| FUTURE | CONDITIONAL |
|---|---|
| je connaîtrai | je connaîtrais |
| tu connaîtras | tu connaîtrais |
| il connaîtra | il connaîtrait |
| nous connaîtrons | nous connaîtrions |
| vous connaîtrez | vous connaîtriez |
| ils connaîtront | ils connaîtraient |

| PRESENT SUBJUNCTIVE | PAST HISTORIC |
|---|---|
| je **connaisse** | je **connus** |
| tu **connaisses** | tu **connus** |
| il **connaisse** | il **connut** |
| nous **connaissions** | nous **connûmes** |
| vous **connaissiez** | vous **connûtes** |
| ils **connaissent** | ils **connurent** |

| **coudre** *to sew* | Auxiliary: **avoir** |
|---|---|

| PAST PARTICIPLE | IMPERATIVE |
|---|---|
| **cousu** | couds |
| | **cousons** |
| | **cousez** |
| PRESENT PARTICIPLE | |
| **cousant** | |

| PRESENT | IMPERFECT |
|---|---|
| je couds | je cousais |
| tu couds | tu cousais |
| il coud | il cousait |
| nous cousons | nous cousions |
| vous cousez | vous cousiez |
| ils cousent | ils cousaient |

| FUTURE | CONDITIONAL |
|---|---|
| je coudrai | je coudrais |
| tu coudras | tu coudrais |
| il coudra | il coudrait |
| nous coudrons | nous coudrions |
| vous coudrez | vous coudriez |
| ils coudront | ils coudraient |

| PRESENT SUBJUNCTIVE | PAST HISTORIC |
|---|---|
| je couse | je cousis |
| tu couses | tu cousis |
| il couse | il cousit |
| nous cousions | nous cousîmes |
| vous cousiez | vous cousîtes |
| ils cousent | ils cousirent |

| **courir** to run | Auxiliary: **avoir** |
|---|---|

**PAST PARTICIPLE**

couru

**PRESENT PARTICIPLE**

courant

**IMPERATIVE**

cours
courons
courez

| PRESENT | | IMPERFECT | |
|---|---|---|---|
| je | cours | je | courais |
| tu | cours | tu | courais |
| il | court | il | courait |
| nous | courons | nous | courions |
| vous | courez | vous | couriez |
| ils | courent | ils | couraient |

| FUTURE | | CONDITIONAL | |
|---|---|---|---|
| je | courrai | je | courrais |
| tu | courras | tu | courrais |
| il | courra | il | courrait |
| nous | courrons | nous | courrions |
| vous | courrez | vous | courriez |
| ils | courront | ils | courraient |

| PRESENT SUBJUNCTIVE | | PAST HISTORIC | |
|---|---|---|---|
| je | coure | je | courus |
| tu | coures | tu | courus |
| il | coure | il | courut |
| nous | courions | nous | courûmes |
| vous | couriez | vous | courûtes |
| ils | courent | ils | coururent |

| **craindre** *to fear* | Auxiliary: **avoir** |
|---|---|

PAST PARTICIPLE

**craint**

PRESENT PARTICIPLE

**craignant**

IMPERATIVE

**crains**
**craignons**
**craignez**

| PRESENT | IMPERFECT |
|---|---|
| je **crains** | je **craignais** |
| tu **crains** | tu **craignais** |
| il **craint** | il **craignait** |
| nous **craignons** | nous **craignions** |
| vous **craignez** | vous **craigniez** |
| ils **craignent** | ils **craignaient** |

| FUTURE | CONDITIONAL |
|---|---|
| je craindrai | je craindrais |
| tu craindras | tu craindrais |
| il craindra | il craindrait |
| nous craindrons | nous craindrions |
| vous craindrez | vous craindriez |
| ils craindront | ils craindraient |

| PRESENT SUBJUNCTIVE | PAST HISTORIC |
|---|---|
| je **craigne** | je **craignis** |
| tu **craignes** | tu **craignis** |
| il **craigne** | il **craignit** |
| nous **craignions** | nous **craignîmes** |
| vous **craigniez** | vous **craignîtes** |
| ils **craignent** | ils **craignirent** |

Verbs ending in **-eindre** and **-oindre** are conjugated similarly

| **croire** to believe | Auxiliary: **avoir** |
|---|---|

PAST PARTICIPLE

**cru**

PRESENT PARTICIPLE

**croyant**

IMPERATIVE

crois
**croyons**
**croyez**

| PRESENT | IMPERFECT |
|---|---|
| je crois | **je croyais** |
| tu crois | **tu croyais** |
| **il croit** | il croyait |
| **nous croyons** | nous croyions |
| **vous croyez** | vous croyiez |
| ils croient | **ils croyaient** |

| FUTURE | CONDITIONAL |
|---|---|
| je croirai | je croirais |
| tu croiras | tu croirais |
| il croira | il croirait |
| nous croirons | nous croirions |
| vous croirez | vous croiriez |
| ils croiront | ils croiraient |

| PRESENT SUBJUNCTIVE | PAST HISTORIC |
|---|---|
| je croie | **je crus** |
| tu croies | **tu crus** |
| il croie | **il crut** |
| **nous croyions** | **nous crûmes** |
| **vous croyiez** | **vous crûtes** |
| ils croient | **ils crurent** |

| **croître** *to grow* | Auxiliary: **avoir** |

PAST PARTICIPLE

**crû**

PRESENT PARTICIPLE

**croissant**

IMPERATIVE

**crois**
**croissons**
**croissez**

| PRESENT | IMPERFECT |
|---|---|
| je **crois** | je **croissais** |
| tu **crois** | tu **croissais** |
| il **croît** | il **croissait** |
| nous **croissons** | nous **croissions** |
| vous **croissez** | vous **croissiez** |
| ils **croissent** | ils **croissaient** |

| FUTURE | CONDITIONAL |
|---|---|
| je croîtrai | je croîtrais |
| tu croîtras | tu croîtrais |
| il croîtra | il croîtrait |
| nous croîtrons | nous croîtrions |
| vous croîtrez | vous croîtriez |
| ils croîtront | ils croîtraient |

| PRESENT SUBJUNCTIVE | PAST HISTORIC |
|---|---|
| je **croisse** | je **crûs** |
| tu **croisses** | tu **crûs** |
| il **croisse** | il **crût** |
| nous **croissions** | nous **crûmes** |
| vous **croissiez** | vous **crûtes** |
| ils **croissent** | ils **crûrent** |

**cueillir** to pick       Auxiliary: **avoir**

PAST PARTICIPLE

cueilli

PRESENT PARTICIPLE

**cueillant**

IMPERATIVE

**cueille
cueillons
cueillez**

| PRESENT | IMPERFECT |
|---|---|
| je **cueille** | je **cueillais** |
| tu **cueilles** | tu **cueillais** |
| il **cueille** | il **cueillait** |
| nous **cueillons** | nous **cueillions** |
| vous **cueillez** | vous **cueilliez** |
| ils **cueillent** | ils **cueillaient** |

| FUTURE | CONDITIONAL |
|---|---|
| je **cueillerai** | je **cueillerais** |
| tu **cueilleras** | tu **cueillerais** |
| il **cueillera** | il **cueillerait** |
| nous **cueillerons** | nous **cueillerions** |
| vous **cueillerez** | vous **cueilleriez** |
| ils **cueilleront** | ils **cueilleraient** |

| PRESENT SUBJUNCTIVE | PAST HISTORIC |
|---|---|
| je **cueille** | je cueillis |
| tu **cueilles** | tu cueillis |
| il **cueille** | il cueillit |
| nous **cueillions** | nous cueillîmes |
| vous **cueilliez** | vous cueillîtes |
| ils **cueillent** | ils cueillirent |

| **cuire** to cook | Auxiliary: **avoir** |
|---|---|

| PAST PARTICIPLE | IMPERATIVE |
|---|---|
| **cuit** | cuis |
| | **cuisons** |
| PRESENT PARTICIPLE | **cuisez** |
| **cuisant** | |

| PRESENT | | IMPERFECT | |
|---|---|---|---|
| je | cuis | **je** | **cuisais** |
| tu | cuis | **tu** | **cuisais** |
| **il** | **cuit** | **il** | **cuisait** |
| **nous** | **cuisons** | **nous** | **cuisions** |
| **vous** | **cuisez** | **vous** | **cuisiez** |
| **ils** | **cuisent** | **ils** | **cuisaient** |

| FUTURE | | CONDITIONAL | |
|---|---|---|---|
| je | cuirai | je | cuirais |
| tu | cuiras | tu | cuirais |
| il | cuira | il | cuirait |
| nous | cuirons | nous | cuirions |
| vous | cuirez | vous | cuiriez |
| ils | cuiront | ils | cuiraient |

| PRESENT SUBJUNCTIVE | | PAST HISTORIC | |
|---|---|---|---|
| **je** | **cuise** | **je** | **cuisis** |
| **tu** | **cuises** | **tu** | **cuisis** |
| **il** | **cuise** | **il** | **cuisit** |
| **nous** | **cuisions** | **nous** | **cuisîmes** |
| **vous** | **cuisiez** | **vous** | **cuisîtes** |
| **ils** | **cuisent** | **ils** | **cuisirent** |

**nuire** to harm, conjugated similarly, but past participle **nui**

| **devoir** _to have to; to owe_ | Auxiliary: **avoir** |
|---|---|

PAST PARTICIPLE

**dû, due**

PRESENT PARTICIPLE

**devant**

IMPERATIVE

**dois**
**devons**
**devez**

| PRESENT | IMPERFECT |
|---|---|
| je **dois** | je **devais** |
| tu **dois** | tu **devais** |
| il **doit** | il **devait** |
| nous **devons** | nous **devions** |
| vous **devez** | vous **deviez** |
| ils **doivent** | ils **devaient** |

| FUTURE | CONDITIONAL |
|---|---|
| je **devrai** | je **devrais** |
| tu **devras** | tu **devrais** |
| il **devra** | il **devrait** |
| nous **devrons** | nous **devrions** |
| vous **devrez** | vous **devriez** |
| ils **devront** | ils **devraient** |

| PRESENT SUBJUNCTIVE | PAST HISTORIC |
|---|---|
| je **doive** | je **dus** |
| tu **doives** | tu **dus** |
| il **doive** | il **dut** |
| nous **devions** | nous **dûmes** |
| vous **deviez** | vous **dûtes** |
| ils **doivent** | ils **durent** |

| **dire** to say, tell | Auxiliary: **avoir** |
|---|---|

| PAST PARTICIPLE | IMPERATIVE |
|---|---|
| **dit** | dis |
| | **disons** |
| | **dites** |
| PRESENT PARTICIPLE | |
| **disant** | |

| PRESENT | | IMPERFECT | |
|---|---|---|---|
| je | dis | **je** | **disais** |
| tu | dis | **tu** | **disais** |
| **il** | **dit** | il | disait |
| **nous** | **disons** | nous | disions |
| **vous** | **dites** | vous | disiez |
| **ils** | **disent** | ils | disaient |

| FUTURE | | CONDITIONAL | |
|---|---|---|---|
| je | dirai | je | dirais |
| tu | diras | tu | dirais |
| il | dira | il | dirait |
| nous | dirons | nous | dirions |
| vous | direz | vous | diriez |
| ils | diront | ils | diraient |

| PRESENT SUBJUNCTIVE | | PAST HISTORIC | |
|---|---|---|---|
| **je** | **dise** | **je** | **dis** |
| **tu** | **dises** | **tu** | **dis** |
| **il** | **dise** | **il** | **dit** |
| **nous** | **disions** | **nous** | **dîmes** |
| **vous** | **disiez** | **vous** | **dîtes** |
| **ils** | **disent** | **ils** | **dirent** |

**interdire** to forbid, conjugated similarly, but 2nd person plural of the present tense is
**vous interdisez**

| **dormir** *to sleep* | Auxiliary: **avoir** |
|---|---|

PAST PARTICIPLE

dormi

PRESENT PARTICIPLE

**dormant**

IMPERATIVE

**dors**
**dormons**
**dormez**

| PRESENT | IMPERFECT |
|---|---|
| je **dors** | je **dormais** |
| tu **dors** | tu **dormais** |
| il **dort** | il **dormait** |
| nous **dormons** | nous **dormions** |
| vous **dormez** | vous **dormiez** |
| ils **dorment** | ils **dormaient** |

| FUTURE | CONDITIONAL |
|---|---|
| je dormirai | je dormirais |
| tu dormiras | tu dormirais |
| il dormira | il dormirait |
| nous dormirons | nous dormirions |
| vous dormirez | vous dormiriez |
| ils dormiront | ils dormiraient |

| PRESENT SUBJUNCTIVE | PAST HISTORIC |
|---|---|
| je **dorme** | je dormis |
| tu **dormes** | tu dormis |
| il **dorme** | il dormit |
| nous **dormions** | nous dormîmes |
| vous **dormiez** | vous dormîtes |
| ils **dorment** | ils dormirent |

| **écrire** to write | Auxiliary: **avoir** |
| --- | --- |

| PAST PARTICIPLE | IMPERATIVE |
| --- | --- |
| **écrit** | écris |
| | **écrivons** |
| | **écrivez** |
| PRESENT PARTICIPLE | |
| **écrivant** | |

| PRESENT | | IMPERFECT | |
| --- | --- | --- | --- |
| | j'écris | | j'écrivais |
| tu | écris | tu | écrivais |
| il | écrit | il | écrivait |
| **nous** | **écrivons** | **nous** | **écrivions** |
| **vous** | **écrivez** | **vous** | **écriviez** |
| **ils** | **écrivent** | **ils** | **écrivaient** |

| FUTURE | | CONDITIONAL | |
| --- | --- | --- | --- |
| | j'écrirai | | j'écrirais |
| tu | écriras | tu | écrirais |
| il | écrira | il | écrirait |
| nous | écrirons | nous | écririons |
| vous | écrirez | vous | écririez |
| ils | écriront | ils | écriraient |

| PRESENT SUBJUNCTIVE | | PAST HISTORIC | |
| --- | --- | --- | --- |
| | j'écrive | | j'écrivis |
| tu | écrives | tu | écrivis |
| il | écrive | il | écrivit |
| nous | écrivions | nous | écrivîmes |
| vous | écriviez | vous | écrivîtes |
| ils | écrivent | ils | écrivirent |

**envoyer** *to send*       Auxiliary: **avoir**

PAST PARTICIPLE              IMPERATIVE

envoyé

                         envoie
                         envoyons
                         envoyez

PRESENT PARTICIPLE

envoyant

| PRESENT | IMPERFECT |
|---|---|
| j'envoie | j'envoyais |
| tu envoies | tu envoyais |
| il envoie | il envoyait |
| nous envoyons | nous envoyions |
| vous envoyez | vous envoyiez |
| ils envoient | ils envoyaient |

| FUTURE | CONDITIONAL |
|---|---|
| **j'enverrai** | **j'enverrais** |
| **tu enverras** | **tu enverrais** |
| **il enverra** | **il enverrait** |
| **nous enverrons** | **nous enverrions** |
| **vous enverrez** | **vous enverriez** |
| **ils enverront** | **ils enverraient** |

| PRESENT SUBJUNCTIVE | PAST HISTORIC |
|---|---|
| j'envoie | j'envoyai |
| tu envoies | tu envoyas |
| il envoie | il envoya |
| nous envoyions | nous envoyâmes |
| vous envoyiez | vous envoyâtes |
| ils envoient | ils envoyèrent |

| **être** to be | Auxiliary: **avoir** |
| --- | --- |

| PAST PARTICIPLE | IMPERATIVE |
| --- | --- |
| été | sois |
| | soyons |
| PRESENT PARTICIPLE | soyez |
| étant | |

| PRESENT | IMPERFECT |
| --- | --- |
| je suis | j'étais |
| tu es | tu étais |
| il est | il était |
| nous sommes | nous étions |
| vous êtes | vous étiez |
| ils sont | ils étaient |

| FUTURE | CONDITIONAL |
| --- | --- |
| je serai | je serais |
| tu seras | tu serais |
| il sera | il serait |
| nous serons | nous serions |
| vous serez | vous seriez |
| ils seront | ils seraient |

| PRESENT SUBJUNCTIVE | PAST HISTORIC |
| --- | --- |
| je sois | je fus |
| tu sois | tu fus |
| il soit | il fut |
| nous soyons | nous fûmes |
| vous soyez | vous fûtes |
| ils soient | ils furent |

| | |
|---|---|
| **faire** *to do; to make* | Auxiliary: **avoir** |

PAST PARTICIPLE

**fait**

PRESENT PARTICIPLE

**faisant**

IMPERATIVE

fais
**faisons**
**faites**

| PRESENT | IMPERFECT |
|---|---|
| je fais | je **faisais** |
| tu fais | tu **faisais** |
| il **fait** | il **faisait** |
| nous **faisons** | nous **faisions** |
| vous **faites** | vous **faisiez** |
| ils **font** | ils **faisaient** |

| FUTURE | CONDITIONAL |
|---|---|
| je **ferai** | je **ferais** |
| tu **feras** | tu **ferais** |
| il **fera** | il **ferait** |
| nous **ferons** | nous **ferions** |
| vous **ferez** | vous **feriez** |
| ils **feront** | ils **feraient** |

| PRESENT SUBJUNCTIVE | PAST HISTORIC |
|---|---|
| je **fasse** | je **fis** |
| tu **fasses** | tu **fis** |
| il **fasse** | il **fit** |
| nous **fassions** | nous **fîmes** |
| vous **fassiez** | vous **fîtes** |
| ils **fassent** | ils **firent** |

| **falloir** _to be necessary_ | Auxiliary: **avoir** |
|---|---|

PAST PARTICIPLE

**fallu**

IMPERATIVE

_not used_

PRESENT PARTICIPLE

_not used_

| PRESENT | IMPERFECT |
|---|---|
| il  faut | il  fallait |

| FUTURE | CONDITIONAL |
|---|---|
| il  faudra | il  faudrait |

| PRESENT SUBJUNCTIVE | PAST HISTORIC |
|---|---|
| il  faille | il  fallut |

| **fuir** *to flee* | Auxiliary: **avoir** |
|---|---|

| PAST PARTICIPLE | IMPERATIVE |
|---|---|
| fui | fuis |
| | **fuyons** |
| | **fuyez** |
| PRESENT PARTICIPLE | |
| **fuyant** | |

| PRESENT | IMPERFECT |
|---|---|
| je fuis | **je fuyais** |
| tu fuis | **tu fuyais** |
| il fuit | **il fuyait** |
| **nous fuyons** | **nous fuyions** |
| **vous fuyez** | **vous fuyiez** |
| **ils fuient** | **ils fuyaient** |

| FUTURE | CONDITIONAL |
|---|---|
| je fuirai | je fuirais |
| tu fuiras | tu fuirais |
| il fuira | il fuirait |
| nous fuirons | nous fuirions |
| vous fuirez | vous fuiriez |
| ils fuiront | ils fuiraient |

| PRESENT SUBJUNCTIVE | PAST HISTORIC |
|---|---|
| **je fuie** | je fuis |
| **tu fuies** | tu fuis |
| **il fuie** | il fuit |
| **nous fuyions** | nous fuîmes |
| **vous fuyiez** | vous fuîtes |
| **ils fuient** | ils fuirent |

| **haïr** *to hate* | Auxiliary: **avoir** |

PAST PARTICIPLE

**haï**

PRESENT PARTICIPLE

**haïssant**

IMPERATIVE

hais
**haïssons**
**haïssez**

| PRESENT | IMPERFECT |
|---|---|
| je hais | je haïssais |
| tu hais | tu haïssais |
| il hait | il haïssait |
| nous haïssons | nous haïssions |
| vous haïssez | vous haïssiez |
| ils haïssent | ils haïssaient |

| FUTURE | CONDITIONAL |
|---|---|
| je haïrai | je haïrais |
| tu haïras | tu haïrais |
| il haïra | il haïrait |
| nous haïrons | nous haïrions |
| vous haïrez | vous haïriez |
| ils haïront | ils haïraient |

| PRESENT SUBJUNCTIVE | PAST HISTORIC |
|---|---|
| je haïsse | je haïs |
| tu haïsses | tu haïs |
| il haïsse | il haït |
| nous haïssions | nous haïmes |
| vous haïssiez | vous haïtes |
| ils haïssent | ils haïrent |

**lire** *to read*        Auxiliary: **avoir**

PAST PARTICIPLE            IMPERATIVE

**lu**

                lis
                lisons
                lisez

PRESENT PARTICIPLE

**lisant**

| PRESENT | IMPERFECT |
|---|---|
| je lis | **je lisais** |
| tu lis | **tu lisais** |
| **il lit** | **il lisait** |
| **nous lisons** | **nous lisions** |
| **vous lisez** | **vous lisiez** |
| **ils lisent** | **ils lisaient** |

| FUTURE | CONDITIONAL |
|---|---|
| je lirai | je lirais |
| tu liras | tu lirais |
| il lira | il lirait |
| nous lirons | nous lirions |
| vous lirez | vous liriez |
| ils liront | ils liraient |

| PRESENT SUBJUNCTIVE | PAST HISTORIC |
|---|---|
| **je lise** | **je lus** |
| **tu lises** | **tu lus** |
| **il lise** | **il lut** |
| **nous lisions** | **nous lûmes** |
| **vous lisiez** | **vous lûtes** |
| **ils lisent** | **ils lurent** |

| **mettre** *to put* | Auxiliary: **avoir** |
|---|---|

| PAST PARTICIPLE | IMPERATIVE |
|---|---|
| **mis** | **mets** |
| | mettons |
| PRESENT PARTICIPLE | mettez |
| mettant | |

| PRESENT | | IMPERFECT | |
|---|---|---|---|
| **je** | **mets** | je | mettais |
| **tu** | **mets** | tu | mettais |
| **il** | **met** | il | mettait |
| nous | mettons | nous | mettions |
| vous | mettez | vous | mettiez |
| ils | mettent | ils | mettaient |

| FUTURE | | CONDITIONAL | |
|---|---|---|---|
| je | mettrai | je | mettrais |
| tu | mettras | tu | mettrais |
| il | mettra | il | mettrait |
| nous | mettrons | nous | mettrions |
| vous | mettrez | vous | mettriez |
| ils | mettront | ils | mettraient |

| PRESENT SUBJUNCTIVE | | PAST HISTORIC | |
|---|---|---|---|
| je | mette | **je** | **mis** |
| tu | mettes | **tu** | **mis** |
| il | mette | **il** | **mit** |
| nous | mettions | **nous** | **mîmes** |
| vous | mettiez | **vous** | **mîtes** |
| ils | mettent | **ils** | **mirent** |

| **moudre** *to grind* | Auxiliary: **avoir** |
|---|---|

| PAST PARTICIPLE | IMPERATIVE |
|---|---|
| **moulu** | mouds |
| | **moulons** |
| | **moulez** |
| PRESENT PARTICIPLE | |
| **moulant** | |

| PRESENT | IMPERFECT |
|---|---|
| je mouds | **je moulais** |
| tu mouds | **tu moulais** |
| il moud | **il moulait** |
| **nous moulons** | **nous moulions** |
| **vous moulez** | **vous mouliez** |
| **ils moulent** | **ils moulaient** |

| FUTURE | CONDITIONAL |
|---|---|
| je moudrai | je moudrais |
| tu moudras | tu moudrais |
| il moudra | il moudrait |
| nous moudrons | nous moudrions |
| vous moudrez | vous moudriez |
| ils moudront | ils moudraient |

| PRESENT SUBJUNCTIVE | PAST HISTORIC |
|---|---|
| **je moule** | **je moulus** |
| **tu moules** | **tu moulus** |
| **il moule** | **il moulut** |
| **nous moulions** | **nous moulûmes** |
| **vous mouliez** | **vous moulûtes** |
| **ils moulent** | **ils moulurent** |

| **mourir** *to die* | Auxiliary: **être** |
|---|---|

PAST PARTICIPLE

**mort**

PRESENT PARTICIPLE

**mourant**

IMPERATIVE

**meurs**
**mourons**
**mourez**

| PRESENT | IMPERFECT |
|---|---|
| je **meurs** | je **mourais** |
| tu **meurs** | tu **mourais** |
| il **meurt** | il **mourait** |
| nous **mourons** | nous **mourions** |
| vous **mourez** | vous **mouriez** |
| ils **meurent** | ils **mouraient** |
| FUTURE | CONDITIONAL |
| je **mourrai** | je **mourrais** |
| tu **mourras** | tu **mourrais** |
| il **mourra** | il **mourrait** |
| nous **mourrons** | nous **mourrions** |
| vous **mourrez** | vous **mourriez** |
| ils **mourront** | ils **mourraient** |
| PRESENT SUBJUNCTIVE | PAST HISTORIC |
| je **meure** | je **mourus** |
| tu **meures** | tu **mourus** |
| il **meure** | il **mourut** |
| nous **mourions** | nous **mourûmes** |
| vous **mouriez** | vous **mourûtes** |
| ils **meurent** | ils **moururent** |

| **naître** to be born | Auxiliary: **être** |
|---|---|

| PAST PARTICIPLE | IMPERATIVE |
|---|---|
| **né** | **nais** |
| | **naissons** |
| PRESENT PARTICIPLE | **naissez** |
| **naissant** | |

| PRESENT | | IMPERFECT | |
|---|---|---|---|
| je | **nais** | je | **naissais** |
| tu | **nais** | tu | **naissais** |
| il | naît | il | naissait |
| nous | **naissons** | nous | naissions |
| vous | **naissez** | vous | naissiez |
| ils | **naissent** | ils | naissaient |

| FUTURE | | CONDITIONAL | |
|---|---|---|---|
| je | naîtrai | je | naîtrais |
| tu | naîtras | tu | naîtrais |
| il | naîtra | il | naîtrait |
| nous | naîtrons | nous | naîtrions |
| vous | naîtrez | vous | naîtriez |
| ils | naîtront | ils | naîtraient |

| PRESENT SUBJUNCTIVE | | PAST HISTORIC | |
|---|---|---|---|
| je | **naisse** | je | naquis |
| tu | **naisses** | tu | naquis |
| il | **naisse** | il | naquit |
| nous | **naissions** | nous | naquîmes |
| vous | **naissiez** | vous | naquîtes |
| ils | **naissent** | ils | naquirent |

| **ouvrir** to open | Auxiliary: **avoir** |
|---|---|

PAST PARTICIPLE

**ouvert**

PRESENT PARTICIPLE

**ouvrant**

IMPERATIVE

**ouvre**
**ouvrons**
**ouvrez**

| PRESENT | IMPERFECT |
|---|---|
| j'ouvre | j'ouvrais |
| tu ouvres | tu ouvrais |
| il ouvre | il ouvrait |
| nous ouvrons | nous ouvrions |
| vous ouvrez | vous ouvriez |
| ils ouvrent | ils ouvraient |

| FUTURE | CONDITIONAL |
|---|---|
| j'ouvrirai | j'ouvrirais |
| tu ouvriras | tu ouvrirais |
| il ouvrira | il ouvrirait |
| nous ouvrirons | nous ouvririons |
| vous ouvrirez | vous ouvririez |
| ils ouvriront | ils ouvriraient |

| PRESENT SUBJUNCTIVE | PAST HISTORIC |
|---|---|
| j'ouvre | j'ouvris |
| tu ouvres | tu ouvris |
| il ouvre | il ouvrit |
| nous ouvrions | nous ouvrîmes |
| vous ouvriez | vous ouvrîtes |
| ils ouvrent | ils ouvrirent |

**offrir** to offer, **souffrir** to suffer are conjugated similarly

| **paraître** *to appear* | Auxiliary: **avoir** |
|---|---|

| PAST PARTICIPLE | IMPERATIVE |
|---|---|
| paru | **parais** |
| | **paraissons** |
| PRESENT PARTICIPLE | **paraissez** |
| paraissant | |

| PRESENT | IMPERFECT |
|---|---|
| je **parais** | je **paraissais** |
| tu **parais** | tu **paraissais** |
| il **paraît** | il **paraissait** |
| nous **paraissons** | nous **paraissions** |
| vous **paraissez** | vous **paraissiez** |
| ils **paraissent** | ils **paraissaient** |

| FUTURE | CONDITIONAL |
|---|---|
| je paraîtrai | je paraîtrais |
| tu paraîtras | tu paraîtrais |
| il paraîtra | il paraîtrait |
| nous paraîtrons | nous paraîtrions |
| vous paraîtrez | vous paraîtriez |
| ils paraîtront | ils paraîtraient |

| PRESENT SUBJUNCTIVE | PAST HISTORIC |
|---|---|
| je **paraisse** | je **parus** |
| tu **paraisses** | tu **parus** |
| il **paraisse** | il **parut** |
| nous **paraissions** | nous **parûmes** |
| vous **paraissiez** | vous **parûtes** |
| ils **paraissent** | ils **parurent** |

| **partir** *to leave* | Auxiliary: **être** |
|---|---|

| PAST PARTICIPLE | IMPERATIVE |
|---|---|
| parti | **pars** |
| | **partons** |
| | **partez** |
| PRESENT PARTICIPLE | |
| **partant** | |

| PRESENT | IMPERFECT |
|---|---|
| je **pars** | je **partais** |
| tu **pars** | tu **partais** |
| il **part** | il **partait** |
| nous **partons** | nous **partions** |
| vous **partez** | vous **partiez** |
| ils **partent** | ils **partaient** |

| FUTURE | CONDITIONAL |
|---|---|
| je partirai | je partirais |
| tu partiras | tu partirais |
| il partira | il partirait |
| nous partirons | nous partirions |
| vous partirez | vous partiriez |
| ils partiront | ils partiraient |

| PRESENT SUBJUNCTIVE | PAST HISTORIC |
|---|---|
| je **parte** | je partis |
| tu **partes** | tu partis |
| il **parte** | il partit |
| nous **partions** | nous partîmes |
| vous **partiez** | vous partîtes |
| ils **partent** | ils partirent |

| **plaire** *to please* | Auxiliary: **avoir** |
|---|---|

PAST PARTICIPLE

**plu**

PRESENT PARTICIPLE

**plaisant**

IMPERATIVE

plais
**plaisons**
**plaisez**

| PRESENT | | IMPERFECT | |
|---|---|---|---|
| je | plais | **je** | **plaisais** |
| tu | plais | **tu** | **plaisais** |
| il | plaît | **il** | **plaisait** |
| nous | plaisons | **nous** | **plaisions** |
| vous | plaisez | **vous** | **plaisiez** |
| ils | plaisent | **ils** | **plaisaient** |

| FUTURE | | CONDITIONAL | |
|---|---|---|---|
| je | plairai | je | plairais |
| tu | plairas | tu | plairais |
| il | plaira | il | plairait |
| nous | plairons | nous | plairions |
| vous | plairez | vous | plairiez |
| ils | plairont | ils | plairaient |

| PRESENT SUBJUNCTIVE | | PAST HISTORIC | |
|---|---|---|---|
| **je** | **plaise** | **je** | **plus** |
| **tu** | **plaises** | **tu** | **plus** |
| **il** | **plaise** | **il** | **plut** |
| **nous** | **plaisions** | **nous** | **plûmes** |
| **vous** | **plaisiez** | **vous** | **plûtes** |
| **ils** | **plaisent** | **ils** | **plurent** |

| **pleuvoir** *to rain* | Auxiliary: **avoir** |
|---|---|

| PAST PARTICIPLE | IMPERATIVE |
|---|---|
| plu | *not used* |

PRESENT PARTICIPLE

**pleuvant**

| PRESENT | IMPERFECT |
|---|---|
| il  pleut | il  pleuvait |

| FUTURE | CONDITIONAL |
|---|---|
| il  pleuvra | il  pleuvrait |

| PRESENT SUBJUNCTIVE | PAST HISTORIC |
|---|---|
| il  pleuve | il  plut |

| **pouvoir** *to be able to* | Auxiliary: **avoir** |
|---|---|

PAST PARTICIPLE

pu

PRESENT PARTICIPLE

pouvant

IMPERATIVE

*not used*

| PRESENT | IMPERFECT |
|---|---|
| je **peux\*** | je **pouvais** |
| tu **peux** | tu **pouvais** |
| il **peut** | il **pouvait** |
| nous **pouvons** | nous **pouvions** |
| vous **pouvez** | vous **pouviez** |
| ils **peuvent** | ils **pouvaient** |

| FUTURE | CONDITIONAL |
|---|---|
| je **pourrai** | je **pourrais** |
| tu **pourras** | tu **pourrais** |
| il **pourra** | il **pourrait** |
| nous **pourrons** | nous **pourrions** |
| vous **pourrez** | vous **pourriez** |
| ils **pourront** | ils **pourraient** |

| PRESENT SUBJUNCTIVE | PAST HISTORIC |
|---|---|
| je **puisse** | je **pus** |
| tu **puisses** | tu **pus** |
| il **puisse** | il **put** |
| nous **puissions** | nous **pûmes** |
| vous **puissiez** | vous **pûtes** |
| ils **puissent** | ils **purent** |

\*In questions: **puis-je?**

| **prendre** to take | Auxiliary: **avoir** |
|---|---|

| PAST PARTICIPLE | IMPERATIVE |
|---|---|
| **pris** | prends |
| | **prenons** |
| PRESENT PARTICIPLE | **prenez** |
| **prenant** | |

| PRESENT | | IMPERFECT | |
|---|---|---|---|
| je | prends | je | prenais |
| tu | prends | tu | prenais |
| il | prend | il | prenait |
| **nous** | **prenons** | **nous** | **prenions** |
| **vous** | **prenez** | **vous** | **preniez** |
| **ils** | **prennent** | **ils** | **prenaient** |

| FUTURE | | CONDITIONAL | |
|---|---|---|---|
| je | prendrai | je | prendrais |
| tu | prendras | tu | prendrais |
| il | prendra | il | prendrait |
| nous | prendrons | nous | prendrions |
| vous | prendrez | vous | prendriez |
| ils | prendront | ils | prendraient |

| PRESENT SUBJUNCTIVE | | PAST HISTORIC | |
|---|---|---|---|
| **je** | **prenne** | je | pris |
| **tu** | **prennes** | tu | pris |
| **il** | **prenne** | il | prit |
| **nous** | **prenions** | **nous** | **prîmes** |
| **vous** | **preniez** | **vous** | **prîtes** |
| **ils** | **prennent** | **ils** | **prirent** |

| **recevoir** to receive | Auxiliary: **avoir** |
|---|---|

PAST PARTICIPLE

reçu

PRESENT PARTICIPLE

recevant

IMPERATIVE

reçois
recevons
recevez

| PRESENT | IMPERFECT |
|---|---|
| je reçois | je recevais |
| tu reçois | tu recevais |
| il reçoit | il recevait |
| nous recevons | nous recevions |
| vous recevez | vous receviez |
| ils reçoivent | ils recevaient |

| FUTURE | CONDITIONAL |
|---|---|
| je recevrai | je recevrais |
| tu recevras | tu recevrais |
| il recevra | il recevrait |
| nous recevrons | nous recevrions |
| vous recevrez | vous recevriez |
| ils recevront | ils recevraient |

| PRESENT SUBJUNCTIVE | PAST HISTORIC |
|---|---|
| je reçoive | je reçus |
| tu reçoives | tu reçus |
| il reçoive | il reçut |
| nous recevions | nous reçûmes |
| vous receviez | vous reçûtes |
| ils reçoivent | ils reçurent |

| **résoudre** *to solve* | Auxiliary: **avoir** |
|---|---|

| PAST PARTICIPLE | IMPERATIVE |
|---|---|
| **résolu** | **résous** |
| | **résolvons** |
| PRESENT PARTICIPLE | **résolvez** |
| **résolvant** | |

| PRESENT | IMPERFECT |
|---|---|
| je **résous** | je **résolvais** |
| tu **résous** | tu **résolvais** |
| il **résout** | il **résolvait** |
| nous **résolvons** | nous **résolvions** |
| vous **résolvez** | vous **résolviez** |
| ils **résolvent** | ils **résolvaient** |

| FUTURE | CONDITIONAL |
|---|---|
| je résoudrai | je résoudrais |
| tu résoudras | tu résoudrais |
| il résoudra | il résoudrait |
| nous résoudrons | nous résoudrions |
| vous résoudrez | vous résoudriez |
| ils résoudront | ils résoudraient |

| PRESENT SUBJUNCTIVE | PAST HISTORIC |
|---|---|
| je **résolve** | je **résolus** |
| tu **résolves** | tu **résolus** |
| il **résolve** | il **résolut** |
| nous **résolvions** | nous **résolûmes** |
| vous **résolviez** | vous **résolûtes** |
| ils **résolvent** | ils **résolurent** |

Grammar

| **rire** to laugh | Auxiliary: **avoir** |

PAST PARTICIPLE

ri

PRESENT PARTICIPLE

riant

IMPERATIVE

ris
rions
riez

| PRESENT | IMPERFECT |
|---|---|
| je ris | je riais |
| tu ris | tu riais |
| **il rit** | il riait |
| nous rions | nous riions |
| vous riez | vous riiez |
| ils rient | ils riaient |

| FUTURE | CONDITIONAL |
|---|---|
| je rirai | je rirais |
| tu riras | tu rirais |
| il rira | il rirait |
| nous rirons | nous ririons |
| vous rirez | vous ririez |
| ils riront | ils riraient |

| PRESENT SUBJUNCTIVE | PAST HISTORIC |
|---|---|
| je rie | **je ris** |
| tu ries | **tu ris** |
| il rie | **il rit** |
| nous riions | **nous rîmes** |
| vous riiez | **vous rîtes** |
| ils rient | **ils rirent** |

| **rompre** *to break* | Auxiliary: **avoir** |
|---|---|

PAST PARTICIPLE

rompu

PRESENT PARTICIPLE

rompant

IMPERATIVE

romps
rompons
rompez

| PRESENT | IMPERFECT |
|---|---|
| je romps | je rompais |
| tu romps | tu rompais |
| **il rompt** | il rompait |
| nous rompons | nous rompions |
| vous rompez | vous rompiez |
| ils rompent | ils rompaient |

| FUTURE | CONDITIONAL |
|---|---|
| je romprai | je romprais |
| tu rompras | tu romprais |
| il rompra | il romprait |
| nous romprons | nous romprions |
| vous romprez | vous rompriez |
| ils rompront | ils rompraient |

| PRESENT SUBJUNCTIVE | PAST HISTORIC |
|---|---|
| je rompe | je rompis |
| tu rompes | tu rompis |
| il rompe | il rompit |
| nous rompions | nous rompîmes |
| vous rompiez | vous rompîtes |
| ils rompent | ils rompirent |

| **savoir** *to know* | Auxiliary: **avoir** |
|---|---|

PAST PARTICIPLE

su

PRESENT PARTICIPLE

sachant

IMPERATIVE

sache
sachons
sachez

| PRESENT | IMPERFECT |
|---|---|
| je **sais** | je **savais** |
| tu **sais** | tu **savais** |
| il **sait** | il **savait** |
| nous **savons** | nous **savions** |
| vous **savez** | vous **saviez** |
| ils **savent** | ils **savaient** |

| FUTURE | CONDITIONAL |
|---|---|
| je **saurai** | je **saurais** |
| tu **sauras** | tu **saurais** |
| il **saura** | il **saurait** |
| nous **saurons** | nous **saurions** |
| vous **saurez** | vous **sauriez** |
| ils **sauront** | ils **sauraient** |

| PRESENT SUBJUNCTIVE | PAST HISTORIC |
|---|---|
| je **sache** | je **sus** |
| tu **saches** | tu **sus** |
| il **sache** | il **sut** |
| nous **sachions** | nous **sûmes** |
| vous **sachiez** | vous **sûtes** |
| ils **sachent** | ils **surent** |

| **sentir** to feel, to smell | Auxiliary: **avoir** |
|---|---|

PAST PARTICIPLE

IMPERATIVE

senti

**sens**
**sentons**
**sentez**

PRESENT PARTICIPLE

**sentant**

| PRESENT | IMPERFECT |
|---|---|
| je **sens** | je **sentais** |
| tu **sens** | tu **sentais** |
| il **sent** | il **sentait** |
| nous **sentons** | nous **sentions** |
| vous **sentez** | vous **sentiez** |
| ils **sentent** | ils **sentaient** |

| FUTURE | CONDITIONAL |
|---|---|
| je sentirai | je sentirais |
| tu sentiras | tu sentirais |
| il sentira | il sentirait |
| nous sentirons | nous sentirions |
| vous sentirez | vous sentiriez |
| ils sentiront | ils sentiraient |

| PRESENT SUBJUNCTIVE | PAST HISTORIC |
|---|---|
| je **sente** | je sentis |
| tu **sentes** | tu sentis |
| il **sente** | il sentit |
| nous **sentions** | nous sentîmes |
| vous **sentiez** | vous sentîtes |
| ils **sentent** | ils sentirent |

| **servir** to serve | Auxiliary: **avoir** |
| --- | --- |

| PAST PARTICIPLE | IMPERATIVE |
| --- | --- |
| servi | **sers**<br>**servons**<br>**servez** |
| PRESENT PARTICIPLE | |
| **servant** | |

| PRESENT | IMPERFECT |
| --- | --- |
| je **sers** | je **servais** |
| tu **sers** | tu **servais** |
| il **sert** | il **servait** |
| nous **servons** | nous **servions** |
| vous **servez** | vous **serviez** |
| ils **servent** | ils **servaient** |

| FUTURE | CONDITIONAL |
| --- | --- |
| je servirai | je servirais |
| tu serviras | tu servirais |
| il servira | il servirait |
| nous servirons | nous servirions |
| vous servirez | vous serviriez |
| ils serviront | ils serviraient |

| PRESENT SUBJUNCTIVE | PAST HISTORIC |
| --- | --- |
| je **serve** | je servis |
| tu **serves** | tu servis |
| il **serve** | il servit |
| nous **servions** | nous servîmes |
| vous **serviez** | vous servîtes |
| ils **servent** | ils servirent |

| **sortir** *to go/come out* | Auxiliary: **être** |
|---|---|

| PAST PARTICIPLE | IMPERATIVE |
|---|---|
| sorti | **sors** |
| | **sortons** |
| PRESENT PARTICIPLE | **sortez** |
| **sortant** | |

| PRESENT | IMPERFECT |
|---|---|
| je **sors** | je **sortais** |
| tu **sors** | tu **sortais** |
| il **sort** | il **sortait** |
| nous **sortons** | nous **sortions** |
| vous **sortez** | vous **sortiez** |
| ils **sortent** | ils **sortaient** |

| FUTURE | CONDITIONAL |
|---|---|
| je sortirai | je sortirais |
| tu sortiras | tu sortirais |
| il sortira | il sortirait |
| nous sortirons | nous sortirions |
| vous sortirez | vous sortiriez |
| ils sortiront | ils sortiraient |

| PRESENT SUBJUNCTIVE | PAST HISTORIC |
|---|---|
| je **sorte** | je sortis |
| tu **sortes** | tu sortis |
| il **sorte** | il sortit |
| nous **sortions** | nous sortîmes |
| vous **sortiez** | vous sortîtes |
| ils **sortent** | ils sortirent |

| **suffire** to be enough | Auxiliary: **avoir** |
|---|---|

| PAST PARTICIPLE | IMPERATIVE |
|---|---|
| **suffi** | suffis |
| | **suffisons** |
| | **suffisez** |
| PRESENT PARTICIPLE | |
| **suffisant** | |

| PRESENT | IMPERFECT |
|---|---|
| je suffis | **je suffisais** |
| tu suffis | **tu suffisais** |
| il suffit | **il suffisait** |
| **nous suffisons** | **nous suffisions** |
| **vous suffisez** | **vous suffisiez** |
| **ils suffisent** | **ils suffisaient** |

| FUTURE | CONDITIONAL |
|---|---|
| je suffirai | je suffirais |
| tu suffiras | tu suffirais |
| il suffira | il suffirait |
| nous suffirons | nous suffirions |
| vous suffirez | vous suffiriez |
| ils suffiront | ils suffiraient |

| PRESENT SUBJUNCTIVE | PAST HISTORIC |
|---|---|
| **je suffise** | **je suffis** |
| **tu suffises** | **tu suffis** |
| **il suffise** | **il suffit** |
| **nous suffisions** | **nous suffîmes** |
| **vous suffisiez** | **vous suffîtes** |
| **ils suffisent** | **ils suffirent** |

| **suivre** *to follow* | Auxiliary: **avoir** |
|---|---|

| PAST PARTICIPLE | IMPERATIVE |
|---|---|
| **suivi** | **suis** |
| | suivons |
| | suivez |
| PRESENT PARTICIPLE | |
| suivant | |

| PRESENT | IMPERFECT |
|---|---|
| **je suis** | je suivais |
| **tu suis** | tu suivais |
| **il suit** | il suivait |
| nous suivons | nous suivions |
| vous suivez | vous suiviez |
| ils suivent | ils suivaient |

| FUTURE | CONDITIONAL |
|---|---|
| je suivrai | je suivrais |
| tu suivras | tu suivrais |
| il suivra | il suivrait |
| nous suivrons | nous suivrions |
| vous suivrez | vous suivriez |
| ils suivront | ils suivraient |

| PRESENT SUBJUNCTIVE | PAST HISTORIC |
|---|---|
| je suive | je suivis |
| tu suives | tu suivis |
| il suive | il suivit |
| nous suivions | nous suivîmes |
| vous suiviez | vous suivîtes |
| ils suivent | ils suivirent |

**se taire** to stop talking                    Auxiliary: **être**

PAST PARTICIPLE                              IMPERATIVE

**tu**                                               tais-toi
                                            **taisons-nous**
                                             **taisez-vous**

PRESENT PARTICIPLE

**se taisant**

| PRESENT | IMPERFECT |
|---------|-----------|
| je me tais | **je me taisais** |
| tu te tais | **tu te taisais** |
| il se tait | **il se taisait** |
| **nous nous taisons** | **nous nous taisions** |
| **vous vous taisez** | **vous vous taisiez** |
| **ils se taisent** | **ils se taisaient** |

| FUTURE | CONDITIONAL |
|--------|-------------|
| je me tairai | je me tairais |
| tu te tairas | tu te tairais |
| il se taira | il se tairait |
| nous nous tairons | nous nous tairions |
| vous vous tairez | vous vous tairiez |
| ils se tairont | ils se tairaient |

| PRESENT SUBJUNCTIVE | PAST HISTORIC |
|---------------------|---------------|
| **je me taise** | **je me tus** |
| **tu te taises** | **tu te tus** |
| **il se taise** | **il se tut** |
| **nous nous taisions** | **nous nous tûmes** |
| **vous vous taisiez** | **vous vous tûtes** |
| **ils se taisent** | **ils se turent** |

| **tenir** to hold | Auxiliary: **avoir** |
|---|---|

PAST PARTICIPLE

**tenu**

PRESENT PARTICIPLE

**tenant**

IMPERATIVE

tiens
tenons
tenez

| PRESENT | IMPERFECT |
|---|---|
| je tiens | je tenais |
| tu tiens | tu tenais |
| il tient | il tenait |
| nous tenons | nous tenions |
| vous tenez | vous teniez |
| ils tiennent | ils tenaient |

| FUTURE | CONDITIONAL |
|---|---|
| je tiendrai | je tiendrais |
| tu tiendras | tu tiendrais |
| il tiendra | il tiendrait |
| nous tiendrons | nous tiendrions |
| vous tiendrez | vous tiendriez |
| ils tiendront | ils tiendraient |

| PRESENT SUBJUNCTIVE | PAST HISTORIC |
|---|---|
| je tienne | je tins |
| tu tiennes | tu tins |
| il tienne | il tint |
| nous tenions | nous tînmes |
| vous teniez | vous tîntes |
| ils tiennent | ils tinrent |

**vaincre** *to defeat* | Auxiliary: **avoir**

PAST PARTICIPLE

vaincu

IMPERATIVE

vaincs
**vainquons**
**vainquez**

PRESENT PARTICIPLE

**vainquant**

| PRESENT | IMPERFECT |
|---|---|
| je vaincs | **je vainquais** |
| tu vaincs | **tu vainquais** |
| il vainc | **il vainquait** |
| **nous vainquons** | **nous vainquions** |
| **vous vainquez** | **vous vainquiez** |
| **ils vainquent** | **ils vainquaient** |

| FUTURE | CONDITIONAL |
|---|---|
| je vaincrai | je vaincrais |
| tu vaincras | tu vaincrais |
| il vaincra | il vaincrait |
| nous vaincrons | nous vaincrions |
| vous vaincrez | vous vaincriez |
| ils vaincront | ils vaincraient |

| PRESENT SUBJUNCTIVE | PAST HISTORIC |
|---|---|
| **je vainque** | **je vainquis** |
| **tu vainques** | **tu vainquis** |
| **il vainque** | **il vainquit** |
| **nous vainquions** | **nous vainquîmes** |
| **vous vainquiez** | **vous vainquîtes** |
| **ils vainquent** | **ils vainquirent** |

| **valoir** _to be worth_ | Auxiliary: **avoir** |
|---|---|

PAST PARTICIPLE

valu

PRESENT PARTICIPLE

valant

IMPERATIVE

vaux
valons
valez

| PRESENT | IMPERFECT |
|---|---|
| je **vaux** | je **valais** |
| tu **vaux** | tu **valais** |
| il **vaut** | il **valait** |
| nous **valons** | nous **valions** |
| vous **valez** | vous **valiez** |
| ils **valent** | ils **valaient** |

| FUTURE | CONDITIONAL |
|---|---|
| je **vaudrai** | je **vaudrais** |
| tu **vaudras** | tu **vaudrais** |
| il **vaudra** | il **vaudrait** |
| nous **vaudrons** | nous **vaudrions** |
| vous **vaudrez** | vous **vaudriez** |
| ils **vaudront** | ils **vaudraient** |

| PRESENT SUBJUNCTIVE | PAST HISTORIC |
|---|---|
| je **vaille** | je **valus** |
| tu **vailles** | tu **valus** |
| il **vaille** | il **valut** |
| nous **valions** | nous **valûmes** |
| vous **valiez** | vous **valûtes** |
| ils **vaillent** | ils **valurent** |

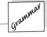

| **venir** *to come* | Auxiliary: **être** |
|---|---|

PAST PARTICIPLE

venu

IMPERATIVE

viens
venons
venez

PRESENT PARTICIPLE

venant

| PRESENT | IMPERFECT |
|---|---|
| je viens | je venais |
| tu viens | tu venais |
| il vient | il venait |
| nous venons | nous venions |
| vous venez | vous veniez |
| ils viennent | ils venaient |

| FUTURE | CONDITIONAL |
|---|---|
| je viendrai | je viendrais |
| tu viendras | tu viendrais |
| il viendra | il viendrait |
| nous viendrons | nous viendrions |
| vous viendrez | vous viendriez |
| ils viendront | ils viendraient |

| PRESENT SUBJUNCTIVE | PAST HISTORIC |
|---|---|
| je vienne | je vins |
| tu viennes | tu vins |
| il vienne | il vint |
| nous venions | nous vînmes |
| vous veniez | vous vîntes |
| ils viennent | ils vinrent |

| **vêtir** *to dress* | Auxiliary: **avoir** |

| PAST PARTICIPLE | IMPERATIVE |
| --- | --- |
| **vêtu** | **vêts** |
| | **vêtons** |
| PRESENT PARTICIPLE | **vêtez** |
| **vêtant** | |

| PRESENT | IMPERFECT |
| --- | --- |
| je **vêts** | je **vêtais** |
| tu **vêts** | tu **vêtais** |
| il **vêt** | il **vêtait** |
| nous **vêtons** | nous **vêtions** |
| vous **vêtez** | vous **vêtiez** |
| ils **vêtent** | ils **vêtaient** |

| FUTURE | CONDITIONAL |
| --- | --- |
| je vêtirai | je vêtirais |
| tu vêtiras | tu vêtirais |
| il vêtira | il vêtirait |
| nous vêtirons | nous vêtirions |
| vous vêtirez | vous vêtiriez |
| ils vêtiront | ils vêtiraient |

| PRESENT SUBJUNCTIVE | PAST HISTORIC |
| --- | --- |
| je **vête** | je vêtis |
| tu **vêtes** | tu vêtis |
| il **vête** | il vêtit |
| nous **vêtions** | nous vêtîmes |
| vous **vêtiez** | vous vêtîtes |
| ils **vêtent** | ils vêtirent |

| **vivre** to live | Auxiliary: **avoir** |
|---|---|

PAST PARTICIPLE

**vécu**

PRESENT PARTICIPLE

**vivant**

IMPERATIVE

**vis**
vivons
vivez

| PRESENT | IMPERFECT |
|---|---|
| **je vis** | je vivais |
| **tu vis** | tu vivais |
| **il vit** | il vivait |
| nous vivons | nous vivions |
| vous vivez | vous viviez |
| ils vivent | ils vivaient |

| FUTURE | CONDITIONAL |
|---|---|
| je vivrai | je vivrais |
| tu vivras | tu vivrais |
| il vivra | il vivrait |
| nous vivrons | nous vivrions |
| vous vivrez | vous vivriez |
| ils vivront | ils vivraient |

| PRESENT SUBJUNCTIVE | PAST HISTORIC |
|---|---|
| je vive | **je vécus** |
| tu vives | **tu vécus** |
| il vive | **il vécut** |
| nous vivions | **nous vécûmes** |
| vous viviez | **vous vécûtes** |
| ils vivent | **ils vécurent** |

| **voir** *to see* | Auxiliary: **avoir** |
|---|---|

PAST PARTICIPLE

**vu**

PRESENT PARTICIPLE

**voyant**

IMPERATIVE

**vois**
**voyons**
**voyez**

| PRESENT | IMPERFECT |
|---|---|
| je **vois** | je **voyais** |
| tu **vois** | tu **voyais** |
| il **voit** | il **voyait** |
| nous **voyons** | nous **voyions** |
| vous **voyez** | vous **voyiez** |
| ils **voient** | ils **voyaient** |

| FUTURE | CONDITIONAL |
|---|---|
| je **verrai** | je **verrais** |
| tu **verras** | tu **verrais** |
| il **verra** | il **verrait** |
| nous **verrons** | nous **verrions** |
| vous **verrez** | vous **verriez** |
| ils **verront** | ils **verraient** |

| PRESENT SUBJUNCTIVE | PAST HISTORIC |
|---|---|
| je **voie** | je **vis** |
| tu **voies** | tu **vis** |
| il **voie** | il **vit** |
| nous **voyions** | nous **vîmes** |
| vous **voyiez** | vous **vîtes** |
| ils **voient** | ils **virent** |

# VERBS: IRREGULAR

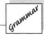

**vouloir** to wish, want                    Auxiliary: **avoir**

PAST PARTICIPLE                              IMPERATIVE

**voulu**

                                       **veuille**
                                    **veuillons**
                                    **veuillez**

PRESENT PARTICIPLE

**voulant**

| PRESENT | IMPERFECT |
|---|---|
| je **veux** | je **voulais** |
| tu **veux** | tu **voulais** |
| il **veut** | il **voulait** |
| nous **voulons** | nous **voulions** |
| vous **voulez** | vous **vouliez** |
| ils **veulent** | ils **voulaient** |

| FUTURE | CONDITIONAL |
|---|---|
| je **voudrai** | je **voudrais** |
| tu **voudras** | tu **voudrais** |
| il **voudra** | il **voudrait** |
| nous **voudrons** | nous **voudrions** |
| vous **voudrez** | vous **voudriez** |
| ils **voudront** | ils **voudraient** |

| PRESENT SUBJUNCTIVE | PAST HISTORIC |
|---|---|
| je **veuille** | je **voulus** |
| tu **veuilles** | tu **voulus** |
| il **veuille** | il **voulut** |
| nous **voulions** | nous **voulûmes** |
| vous **vouliez** | vous **voulûtes** |
| ils **veuillent** | ils **voulurent** |

## ◻ The Gender of Nouns

In French, all nouns are either masculine or feminine, whether denoting people, animals or things. Unlike English, there is no neuter gender for inanimate objects and abstract nouns.

Gender is largely unpredictable and has to be learnt for each noun. However, the following guidelines will help you determine the gender for certain types of nouns.

+ Nouns denoting male people and animals are usually – but not always – masculine, e.g.

| **un homme** | **un taureau** |
|---|---|
| *a man* | *a bull* |
| **un infirmier** | **un cheval** |
| *a (male) nurse* | *a horse* |

+ Nouns denoting female people and animals are usually – but not always – feminine, e.g.

| **une fille** | **une vache** |
|---|---|
| *a girl* | *a cow* |
| **une infirmière** | **une brebis** |
| *a nurse* | *a ewe* |

+ Some nouns are masculine OR feminine depending on the sex of the person to whom they refer, e.g.

| **un camarade** | **une camarade** |
|---|---|
| *a (male) friend* | *a (female) friend* |
| **un Belge** | **une Belge** |
| *a Belgian (man)* | *a Belgian (woman)* |

+ Other nouns referring to either men or women have only one gender which applies to both, e.g.

| **un professeur** | **une personne** | **une sentinelle** |
|---|---|---|
| *a teacher* | *a person* | *a sentry* |
| **un témoin** | **une victime** | **une recrue** |
| *a witness* | *a victim* | *a recruit* |

- Sometimes the ending of the noun indicates its gender. Shown below are some of the most important to guide you:

### Masculine endings

| | |
|---|---|
| **-age** | **le courage** *courage*, **le rinçage** *rinsing* |
| | EXCEPTIONS: **une cage** *a cage*, **une image** *a picture*, **la nage** *swimming*, **une page** *a page*, **une plage** *a beach*, **une rage** *a rage* |
| **-ment** | **le commencement** *the beginning* |
| | EXCEPTION: **une jument** *a mare* |
| **-oir** | **un couloir** *a corridor*, **un miroir** *a mirror* |
| **-sme** | **le pessimisme** *pessimism*, **l'enthousiasme** *enthusiasm* |

### Feminine endings

| | |
|---|---|
| **-ance, anse** | **la confiance** *confidence*, **la danse** *dancing* |
| **-ence, -ense** | **la prudence** *caution*, **la défense** *defence* |
| | EXCEPTION: **le silence** *silence* |
| **-ion** | **une région** *a region*, **une addition** *a bill* |
| | EXCEPTIONS: **un pion** *a pawn*, **un espion** *a spy* |
| **-oire** | **une baignoire** *a bath(tub)* |
| **-té, -tié** | **la beauté** *beauty*, **la moitié** *half* |

- Suffixes which differentiate between male and female are shown on pp 134 and 136.

- The following words have different meanings depending on gender:

| | | | |
|---|---|---|---|
| **le crêpe** | *crêpe* | **la crêpe** | *pancake* |
| **le livre** | *book* | **la livre** | *pound* |
| **le manche** | *handle* | **la manche** | *sleeve* |
| **le mode** | *method* | **la mode** | *fashion* |
| **le moule** | *mould* | **la moule** | *mussel* |
| **le page** | *page(boy)* | **la page** | *page* (in book) |
| **le physique** | *physique* | **la physique** | *physics* |
| **le poêle** | *stove* | **la poêle** | *frying pan* |
| **le somme** | *nap* | **la somme** | *sum* |
| **le tour** | *turn* | **la tour** | *tower* |
| **le voile** | *veil* | **la voile** | *sail* |

## ◻ Gender: the Formation of Feminines

As in English, male and female are sometimes differentiated by the use of two quite separate words, e.g.

| **mon oncle** | **ma tante** |
|---|---|
| *my uncle* | *my aunt* |
| **un taureau** | **une vache** |
| *a bull* | *a cow* |

There are, however, some words in French which show this distinction by the form of their ending.

◆ Some nouns add an **e** to the masculine singular form to form the feminine → ①

◆ If the masculine singular form already ends in **-e**, no further **e** is added in the feminine → ②

◆ Some nouns undergo a further change when **e** is added. These changes occur regularly and are shown on p 136.

**Feminine forms to note**

| MASCULINE | FEMININE | |
|---|---|---|
| un âne | une ânesse | *donkey* |
| le comte | la comtesse | *count/countess* |
| le duc | la duchesse | *duke/duchess* |
| un Esquimau | une Esquimaude | *Eskimo* |
| le fou | la folle | *madman/madwoman* |
| le Grec | la Grecque | *Greek* |
| un hôte | une hôtesse | *host/hostess* |
| le jumeau | la jumelle | *twin* |
| le maître | la maîtresse | *master/mistress* |
| le prince | la princesse | *prince/princess* |
| le tigre | la tigresse | *tiger/tigress* |
| le traître | la traîtresse | *traitor* |
| le Turc | la Turque | *Turk* |
| le vieux | la vieille | *old man/old woman* |

① **un ami**
a (male) friend
**un employé**
a (male) employee
**un Français**
a Frenchman

**une amie**
a (female) friend
**une employée**
a (female) employee
**une Française**
a Frenchwoman

② **un élève**
a (male) pupil
**un collègue**
a (male) colleague
**un camarade**
a (male) friend

**une élève**
a (female) pupil
**une collègue**
a (female) colleague
**une camarade**
a (female) friend

## ◻ **Regular feminine endings**

| MASC. SING. | FEM. SING. | |
|---|---|---|
| -f | -ve | → ① |
| -x | -se | → ② |
| -eur | -euse | → ③ |
| -teur | { -teuse | → ④ |
| | -trice | → ⑤ |

Some nouns double the final consonant before adding **e**:

| MASC. SING. | FEM. SING. | |
|---|---|---|
| -an | -anne | → ⑥ |
| -en | -enne | → ⑦ |
| -on | -onne | → ⑧ |
| -et | -ette | → ⑨ |
| -el | -elle | → ⑩ |

Some nouns add an accent to the final syllable before adding **e**:

| MASC. SING. | FEM. SING. | |
|---|---|---|
| -er | -ère | → ⑪ |

### Pronunciation and feminine endings

This is dealt with on p 244.

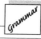
Grammar

| | | |
|---|---|---|
| **1** | **un sportif**<br>a sportsman | **une sportive**<br>a sportswoman |
| | **un veuf**<br>a widower | **une veuve**<br>a widow |
| **2** | **un époux**<br>a husband | **une épouse**<br>a wife |
| | **un amoureux**<br>a man in love | **une amoureuse**<br>a woman in love |
| **3** | **un danseur**<br>a dancer | **une danseuse**<br>a dancer |
| | **un voleur**<br>a thief | **une voleuse**<br>a thief |
| **4** | **un menteur**<br>a liar | **une menteuse**<br>a liar |
| | **un chanteur**<br>a singer | **une chanteuse**<br>a singer |
| **5** | **un acteur**<br>an actor | **une actrice**<br>an actress |
| | **un conducteur**<br>a driver | **une conductrice**<br>a driver |
| **6** | **un paysan**<br>a countryman | **une paysanne**<br>a countrywoman |
| **7** | **un Parisien**<br>a Parisian | **une Parisienne**<br>a Parisian (woman) |
| **8** | **un baron**<br>a baron | **une baronne**<br>a baroness |
| **9** | **le cadet**<br>the youngest (child) | **la cadette**<br>the youngest (child) |
| **10** | **un intellectuel**<br>an intellectual | **une intellectuelle**<br>an intellectual |
| **11** | **un étranger**<br>a foreigner | **une étrangère**<br>a foreigner |
| | **le dernier**<br>the last (one) | **la dernière**<br>the last (one) |

## ◻ The Formation of Plurals

- Most nouns add **s** to the singular form → 1

- When the singular form already ends in **-s**, **-x** or **-z**, no further **s** is added → 2

- For nouns ending in **-au**, **-eau** or **-eu**, the plural ends in **-aux**, **-eaux** or **-eux** → 3

  EXCEPTIONS: | **pneu** | tyre | (plur: **pneus**) |
  | --- | --- | --- |
  | **bleu** | bruise | (plur: **bleus**) |

- For nouns ending in **-al** or **-ail**, the plural ends in **-aux** → 4

  EXCEPTIONS: | **bal** | ball | (plur: **bals**) |
  | --- | --- | --- |
  | **festival** | festival | (plur: **festivals**) |
  | **chandail** | sweater | (plur: **chandails**) |
  | **détail** | detail | (plur: **détails**) |

- Forming the plural of compound nouns is complicated and you are advised to check each one individually in a dictionary.

### Irregular plural forms

- Some masculine nouns ending in **-ou** add **x** in the plural. These are:

| **bijou** | jewel | **genou** | knee | **joujou** | toy |
| --- | --- | --- | --- | --- | --- |
| **caillou** | pebble | **hibou** | owl | **pou** | louse |
| **chou** | cabbage | | | | |

- Some other nouns are totally unpredictable. Chief among these are:

| SINGULAR | | PLURAL |
| --- | --- | --- |
| **œil** | eye | **yeux** |
| **ciel** | sky | **cieux** |
| **Monsieur** | Mr | **Messieurs** |
| **Madame** | Mrs | **Mesdames** |
| **Mademoiselle** | Miss | **Mesdemoiselles** |

### Pronunciation of plural forms

This is dealt with on p 244.

1.  **le jardin**          **les jardins**
    the garden          the gardens
    **une voiture**,     **des voitures**
    a car               (some) cars
    **l'hôtel**          **les hôtels**
    the hotel           the hotels

2.  **un tas**           **des tas**
    a heap              (some) heaps
    **une voix**         **des voix**
    a voice             (some) voices
    **le gaz**           **les gaz**
    the gas             the gases

3.  **un tuyau**         **des tuyaux**
    a pipe              (some) pipes
    **le chapeau**       **les chapeaux**
    the hat             the hats
    **le feu**           **les feux**
    the fire            the fires

4.  **le journal**       **les journaux**
    the newspaper       the newspapers
    **un travail**       **des travaux**
    a job               (some) jobs

# ARTICLES

## ❏ The Definite Article

|  | WITH MASC. NOUN | WITH FEM. NOUN |  |
|---|---|---|---|
| SING. | le (l') | la (l') | *the* |
| PLUR. | les | les | *the* |

- The gender and number of the noun determines the form of the article → ①

- **le** and **la** change to **l'** before a vowel or an **h** 'mute' → ②

- For uses of the definite article see p 142.

- **à + le/la (l'), à + les**

|  | WITH MASC. NOUN | WITH FEM. NOUN |  |
|---|---|---|---|
| SING. | au (à l') | à la (à l') | → ③ |
| PLUR. | aux | aux |  |

- The definite article combines with the preposition **à**, as shown above. You should pay particular attention to the masculine singular form **au,** and both plural forms **aux,** since these are not visually the sum of their parts.

- **de + le/la (l'), de + les**

|  | WITH MASC. NOUN | WITH FEM. NOUN |  |
|---|---|---|---|
| SING. | du (de l') | de la (de l') | → ④ |
| PLUR. | des | des |  |

- The definite article combines with the preposition **de**, as shown above. You should pay particular attention to the masculine singular form **du**, and both plural forms **des**, since these are not visually the sum of their parts.

| MASCULINE | FEMININE |
|---|---|
| **1** **le train**<br>the train | **la gare**<br>the station |
| **le garçon**<br>the boy | **la fille**<br>the girl |
| **les hôtels**<br>the hotels | **les écoles**<br>the schools |
| **les professeurs**<br>the teachers | **les femmes**<br>the women |
| **2** **l'acteur**<br>the actor | **l'actrice**<br>the actress |
| **l'effet**<br>the effect | **l'eau**<br>the water |
| **l'ingrédient**<br>the ingredient | **l'idée**<br>the idea |
| **l'objet**<br>the object | **l'ombre**<br>the shadow |
| **l'univers**<br>the universe | **l'usine**<br>the factory |
| **l'hôpital**<br>the hospital | **l'heure**<br>the time |
| **3** **au cinéma**<br>at/to the cinema | **à la bibliothèque**<br>at/to the library |
| **à l'employé**<br>to the employee | **à l'infirmière**<br>to the nurse |
| **à l'hôpital**<br>at/to the hospital | **à l'hôtesse**<br>to the hostess |
| **aux étudiants**<br>to the students | **aux maisons**<br>to the houses |
| **4** **du bureau**<br>from/of the office | **de la réunion**<br>from/of the meeting |
| **de l'auteur**<br>from/of the author | **de l'Italienne**<br>from/of the Italian woman |
| **de l'hôte**<br>from/of the host | **de l'horloge**<br>of the clock |
| **des États-Unis**<br>from/of the United States | **des vendeuses**<br>from/of the saleswomen |

## ◻ Uses of the Definite Article

While the definite article is used in much the same way in French as it is in English, its use is more widespread in French. Unlike English the definite article is also used:

- with abstract nouns, except when following certain prepositions → ①

- in generalizations, especially with plural or uncountable* nouns → ②

- with names of countries → ③
  EXCEPTIONS: no article with countries following **en** *to/in* → ④

- with parts of the body → ⑤
  'Ownership' is often indicated by an indirect object pronoun or a reflexive pronoun → ⑥

- in expressions of quantity/rate/price → ⑦

- with titles/ranks/professions followed by a proper name → ⑧

- The definite article is NOT used with nouns in apposition → ⑨

*An uncountable noun is one which cannot be used in the plural or with an indefinite article, e.g. **l'acier** *steel*, **le lait** *milk*.

| | | |
|---|---|---|
| **1** | **Les prix montent** | |
| | Prices are rising | |
| | **L'amour rayonne dans ses yeux** | |
| | Love shines in his eyes | |
| | BUT     **avec plaisir** | **sans espoir** |
| |          with pleasure | without hope |
| **2** | **Je n'aime pas le café** | |
| | I don't like coffee | |
| | **Les enfants ont besoin d'être aimés** | |
| | Children need to be loved | |
| **3** | **le Japon**    **la France** | **l'Italie**    **les Pays-Bas** |
| | Japan        France | Italy       The Netherlands |
| **4** | **aller en Écosse** | **Il travaille en Allemagne** |
| | to go to Scotland | He works in Germany |
| **5** | **Tournez la tête à gauche** | |
| | Turn your head to the left | |
| | **j'ai mal à la gorge** | |
| | My throat is sore, I have a sore throat | |
| **6** | **La tête me tourne** | |
| | My head is spinning | |
| | **Elle s'est brossé les dents** | |
| | She brushed her teeth | |
| **7** | **40 francs le mètre/le kilo/la douzaine/la pièce** | |
| | 40 francs a metre/a kilo/a dozen/each | |
| | **rouler à 80 km à l'heure** | |
| | to go at 50 m.p.h. | |
| | **payé à l'heure/au jour/au mois** | |
| | paid by the hour/by the day/by the month | |
| **8** | **le roi Georges III** | **le capitaine Darbeau** |
| | King George III | Captain Darbeau |
| | **le docteur Rousseau** | **Monsieur le président** |
| | Dr Rousseau | Mr Chairman/President |
| **9** | **Victor Hugo, grand écrivain du dix-neuvième siècle** | |
| | Victor Hugo, a great author of the nineteenth century | |
| | **Joseph Leblanc, inventeur et entrepreneur, a été le premier ...** | |
| | Joseph Leblanc, an inventor and entrepreneur, was the first ... | |

## ◻ **The Partitive Article**

The partitive article has the sense of *some* or *any*, although the French is not always translated in English.

### Forms of the partitive

|  | WITH MASC. NOUN | WITH FEM. NOUN |  |
|---|---|---|---|
| SING. | **du (de l')** | **de la (de l')** | *some, any* |
| PLUR. | **des** | **des** | *some, any* |

- The gender and number of the noun determines the form of the partitive → 1

- The forms shown in brackets are used before a vowel or an **h** 'mute' → 2

- **des** becomes **de** (**d'** + vowel) before an adjective → 3, unless the adjective and noun are seen as forming one unit → 4

- In negative sentences **de** (**d'** + vowel) is used for both genders, singular and plural → 5

  EXCEPTION: after **ne ... que** *only*, the positive forms above are used → 6

**1**    **Avez-vous du sucre?**
Have you any sugar?
**J'ai acheté de la farine et de la margarine**
I bought (some) flour and margarine
**Il a mangé des gâteaux**
He ate some cakes
**Est-ce qu'il y a des lettres pour moi?**
Are there (any) letters for me?

**2**    **Il me doit de l'argent**
He owes me (some) money
**C'est de l'histoire ancienne**
That's ancient history

**3**    **Il a fait de gros efforts pour nous aider**
He made a great effort to help us
**Cette région a de belles églises**
This region has some beautiful churches

**4**    **des grandes vacances**      **des jeunes gens**
summer holidays          young people

**5**    **Je n'ai pas de nourriture/d'argent**
I don't have any food/money
**Vous n'avez pas de timbres/d'œufs?**
Have you no stamps/eggs?
**Je ne mange jamais de viande/d'omelettes**
I never eat meat/omelettes
**Il ne veut plus de visiteurs/d'eau**
He doesn't want any more visitors/water

**6**    **Il ne boit que du thé/de la bière/de l'eau**
He only drinks tea/beer/water
**Je n'ai que des problèmes avec cette machine**
I have nothing but problems with this machine

## ◻ The Indefinite Article

|  | WITH<br>MASC. NOUN | WITH<br>FEM. NOUN |  |
|---|---|---|---|
| SING. | **un** | **une** | *a* |
| PLUR. | **des** | **des** | *some* |

◆ **des** is also the plural of the partitive article (see p 144).

◆ In negative sentences, **de** (**d'** + vowel) is used for both singular and plural → 1

◆ The indefinite article is used in French largely as it is in English EXCEPT:

- there is no article when a person's profession is being stated → 2
  The article *is* present however, following **ce** (**c'** + vowel) → 3

- the English article is not translated by **un/une** in constructions like *what a surprise, what an idiot* → 4

- in structures of the type given in example 5 the article **un/une** is used in French and not translated in English → 5

1. **Je n'ai pas de livre/d'enfants**
   I don't have a book/(any) children

2. **Il est professeur**        **Ma mère est infirmière**
   He's a teacher          My mother's a nurse

3. **C'est un médecin**        **Ce sont des acteurs**
   He's/She's a doctor       They're actors

4. **Quelle surprise!**        **Quel dommage!**
   What a surprise!          What a shame!

5. **avec une grande sagesse/un courage admirable**
   with great wisdom /admirable courage
   **Il a fait preuve d'un sang-froid incroyable**
   He showed incredible coolness
   **Un produit d'une qualité incomparable**
   A product of incomparable quality

Grammar

## ❑ Adjectives

Most adjectives agree in number and in gender with the noun or pronoun.

### The formation of feminines

+ Most adjectives add an **e** to the masculine singular form → 1
+ If the masculine singular form already ends in **-e**, no further **e** is added → 2
+ Some adjectives undergo a further change when **e** is added. These changes occur regularly and are shown on p 150.
+ Irregular feminine forms are shown on p 152.

### The formation of plurals

+ The plural of both regular and irregular adjectives is formed by adding an **s** to the masculine or feminine singular form, as appropriate → 3
+ When the masculine singular form already ends in **-s** or **-x**, no further **s** is added → 4
+ For masculine singulars ending in **-au** and **-eau**, the masculine plural is **-aux** and **-eaux** → 5
+ For masculine singulars ending in **-al**, the masculine plural is **-aux** → 6

| EXCEPTIONS: | **final** | (masculine plural **finals**) |
| | **fatal** | (masculine plural **fatals**) |
| | **naval** | (masculine plural **navals**) |

### Pronunciation of feminine and plural adjectives

This is dealt with on p 244.

| | | |
|---|---|---|
| 1 | **mon frère aîné**<br>my elder brother | **ma sœur aînée**<br>my elder sister |
| | **le petit garçon**<br>the little boy | **la petite fille**<br>the little girl |
| | **un sac gris**<br>a grey bag | **une chemise grise**<br>a grey shirt |
| | **un bruit fort**<br>a loud noise | **une voix forte**<br>a loud voice |
| 2 | **un jeune homme**<br>a young man | **une jeune femme**<br>a young woman |
| | **l'autre verre**<br>the other glass | **l'autre assiette**<br>the other plate |
| 3 | **le dernier train**<br>the last train | **les derniers trains**<br>the last trains |
| | **une vieille maison**<br>an old house | **de vieilles maisons**<br>old houses |
| | **un long voyage**<br>a long journey | **de longs voyages**<br>long journeys |
| | **la rue étroite**<br>the narrow street | **les rues étroites**<br>the narrow streets |
| 4 | **un diplomate français**<br>a French diplomat | **des diplomates français**<br>French diplomats |
| | **un homme dangereux**<br>a dangerous man | **des hommes dangereux**<br>dangerous men |
| 5 | **le nouveau professeur**<br>the new teacher | **les nouveaux professeurs**<br>the new teachers |
| | **un chien esquimau**<br>a husky (Fr. = an Eskimo dog) | **des chiens esquimaux**<br>huskies (Fr. = Eskimo dogs) |
| 6 | **un ami loyal**<br>a loyal friend | **des amis loyaux**<br>loyal friends |
| | **un geste amical**<br>a friendly gesture | **des gestes amicaux**<br>friendly gestures |

## ◻ Regular feminine endings

| MASC. SING. | FEM. SING. | EXAMPLES | |
|---|---|---|---|
| -f | -ve | neuf, vif | → 1 |
| -x | -se | heureux, jaloux | → 2 |
| -eur | -euse | travailleur, flâneur | → 3 |
| -teur | { -teuse | flatteur, menteur | → 4 |
| | -trice | destructeur, séducteur | → 5 |

EXCEPTIONS:

> **bref**: see p 152
> **doux, faux, roux, vieux**: see p 152
> **extérieur, inférieur, intérieur, meilleur, supérieur**: all add **e** to the masculine
> **enchanteur**: fem. = **enchanteresse**

| MASC. SING. | FEM. SING. | EXAMPLES | |
|---|---|---|---|
| -an | -anne | paysan | → 6 |
| -en | -enne | ancien, parisien | → 7 |
| -on | -onne | bon, breton | → 8 |
| -as | -asse | bas, las | → 9 |
| -et* | -ette | muet, violet | → 10 |
| -el | -elle | annuel, mortel | → 11 |
| -eil | -eille | pareil, vermeil | → 12 |

EXCEPTION:

> **ras**: fem. = **rase**

| MASC. SING. | FEM. SING. | EXAMPLES | |
|---|---|---|---|
| -et* | -ète | secret, complet | → 13 |
| -er | -ère | étranger, fier | → 14 |

*Note that there are two feminine endings for masculine adjectives ending in **-et**.

| | | |
|---|---|---|
| 1 | **un résultat positif**<br>a positive result | **une attitude positive**<br>a positive attitude |
| 2 | **d'un ton sérieux**<br>in a serious tone (of voice) | **une voix sérieuse**<br>a serious voice |
| 3 | **un enfant trompeur**<br>a deceitful child | **une déclaration trompeuse**<br>a misleading statement |
| 4 | **un tableau flatteur**<br>a flattering picture | **une comparaison flatteuse**<br>a flattering comparison |
| 5 | **un geste protecteur**<br>a protective gesture | **une couche protectrice**<br>a protective layer |
| 6 | **un problème paysan**<br>a farming problem | **la vie paysanne**<br>country life |
| 7 | **un avion égyptien**<br>an Egyptian plane | **une statue égyptienne**<br>an Egyptian statue |
| 8 | **un bon repas**<br>a good meal | **de bonne humeur**<br>in a good mood |
| 9 | **un plafond bas**<br>a low ceiling | **à voix basse**<br>in a low voice |
| 10 | **un travail net**<br>a clean piece of work | **une explication nette**<br>a clear explanation |
| 11 | **un homme cruel**<br>a cruel man | **une remarque cruelle**<br>a cruel remark |
| 12 | **un livre pareil**<br>such a book | **en pareille occasion**<br>on such an occasion |
| 13 | **un regard inquiet**<br>an anxious look | **une attente inquiète**<br>an anxious wait |
| 14 | **un goût amer**<br>a bitter taste | **une amère déception**<br>a bitter disappointment |

## ☐ Adjectives with irregular feminine forms

| MASC. SING. | FEM. SING. | | |
|---|---|---|---|
| aigu | aiguë | sharp; high-pitched | → 1 |
| ambigu | ambiguë | ambiguous | |
| beau (bel)* | belle | beautiful | |
| bénin | bénigne | benign | |
| blanc | blanche | white | |
| bref | brève | brief, short | → 2 |
| doux | douce | soft; sweet | |
| épais | épaisse | thick | |
| esquimau | esquimaude | Eskimo | |
| faux | fausse | wrong | |
| favori | favorite | favourite | → 3 |
| fou (fol)* | folle | mad | |
| frais | fraîche | fresh | → 4 |
| franc | franche | frank | |
| gentil | gentille | kind | |
| grec | grecque | Greek | |
| gros | grosse | big | |
| jumeau | jumelle | twin | → 5 |
| long | longue | long | |
| malin | maligne | malignant | |
| mou (mol)* | molle | soft | |
| nouveau (nouvel)* | nouvelle | new | |
| nul | nulle | no | |
| public | publique | public | → 6 |
| roux | rousse | red-haired | |
| sec | sèche | dry | |
| sot | sotte | foolish | |
| turc | turque | Turkish | |
| vieux (vieil)* | vieille | old | |

*This form is used when the following word begins with a vowel or an
h 'mute' → 7

1. **un son aigu**
   a high-pitched sound

   **une douleur aiguë**
   a sharp pain

2. **un bref discours**
   a short speech

   **une brève rencontre**
   a short meeting

3. **mon sport favori**
   my favourite sport

   **ma chanson favorite**
   my favourite song

4. **du pain frais**
   fresh bread

   **de la crème fraîche**
   fresh cream

5. **mon frère jumeau**
   my twin brother

   **ma sœur jumelle**
   my twin sister

6. **un jardin public**
   a (public) park

   **l'opinion publique**
   public opinion

7. **un bel appartement**
   a beautiful flat
   **le nouvel inspecteur**
   the new inspector
   **un vieil arbre**
   an old tree

   **un bel habit**
   a beautiful outfit
   **un nouvel harmonica**
   a new harmonica
   **un vieil hôtel**
   an old hotel

## ❑ Comparatives and Superlatives

### Comparatives

These are formed using the following constructions:

| | | |
|---|---|---|
| **plus ... (que)** | *more ... (than)* | → 1 |
| **moins ... (que)** | *less ... (than)* | → 2 |
| **aussi ... que** | *as ... as* | → 3 |
| **si ... que\*** | *as ... as* | → 4 |

\*used mainly after a negative

### Superlatives

These are formed using the following constructions:

| | | |
|---|---|---|
| **le/la/les plus ... (que)** | *the most ... (that)* | → 5 |
| **le/la/les moins ... (que)** | *the least ... (that)* | → 6 |

- When the possessive adjective is present, two constructions are possible → 7
- After a superlative the preposition **de** is often translated as *in* → 8
- If a clause follows a superlative, the verb is in the subjunctive → 9

### Adjectives with irregular comparatives/superlatives

| ADJECTIVE | COMPARATIVE | SUPERLATIVE |
|---|---|---|
| **bon** | **meilleur** | **le meilleur** |
| *good* | *better* | *the best* |
| **mauvais** | **pire** OR | **le pire** OR |
| *bad* | **plus mauvais** | **le plus mauvais** |
| | *worse* | *the worst* |
| **petit** | **moindre\*** OR | **le moindre\*** OR |
| *small* | **plus petit** | **le plus petit** |
| | *smaller;* | *the smallest;* |
| | *lesser* | *the least* |

\*used only with abstract nouns

- Comparative and superlative adjectives agree in number and in gender with the noun, just like any other adjective → 10

1. **une raison plus grave**
   a more serious reason
   **Elle est plus petite que moi**
   She is smaller than me

2. **un film moins connu**
   a less well-known film
   **C'est moins cher qu'il ne pense**
   It's cheaper than he thinks

3. **Robert était aussi inquiet que moi**
   Robert was as worried as I was
   **Cette ville n'est pas aussi grande que Bordeaux**
   This town isn't as big as Bordeaux

4. **Ils ne sont pas si contents que ça**
   They aren't as happy as all that

5. **le guide le plus utile**      **la voiture la plus petite**
   the most useful guidebook      the smallest car
   **les plus grandes maisons**
   the biggest houses

6. **le mois le moins agréable**      **la fille la moins forte**
   the least pleasant month      the weakest girl
   **les moins belles peintures**
   the least attractive paintings

7. **Mon désir le plus cher** ⎫
   **Mon plus cher désir**    ⎬ **est de voyager**
   My dearest wish is to travel

8. **la plus grande gare de Londres**
   the biggest station in London
   **l'habitant le plus âgé du village/de la région**
   the oldest inhabitant in the village/in the area

9. **la personne la plus gentille que je connaisse**
   the nicest person I know

10. **les moindres difficultés**
    the least difficulties
    **la meilleure qualité**
    the best quality

## ❏ Demonstrative Adjectives

|        | MASCULINE | FEMININE |              |
|--------|-----------|----------|--------------|
| SING.  | **ce (cet)** | **cette** | *this; that* |
| PLUR.  | **ces**   | **ces**  | *these; those* |

♦ Demonstrative adjectives agree in number and gender with the noun → ①

♦ **cet** is used when the following word begins with a vowel or an **h** 'mute' → ②

♦ For emphasis or in order to distinguish between people or objects, **-ci** or **-là** is added to the noun: **-ci** indicates proximity (usually translated *this*) and **là** distance *(that)* → ③

① **Ce stylo ne marche pas**
This/That pen isn't working
**Comment s'appelle cette entreprise?**
What's this/that company called?
**Ces livres sont les miens**
These/Those books are mine
**Ces couleurs sont plus jolies**
These/Those colours are nicer

② **cet oiseau**
this/that bird
**cet article**
this/that article
**cet homme**
this/that man

③ **Combien coûte ce manteau-ci?**
How much is this coat?
**Je voudrais cinq de ces pommes-là**
I'd like five of those apples
**Est-ce que tu reconnais cette personne-là?**
Do you recognize that person?
**Mettez ces vêtements-ci dans cette valise-là**
Put these clothes in that case
**Ce garçon-là appartient à ce groupe-ci**
That boy belongs to this group

## ❑ Interrogative Adjectives

|  | MASCULINE | FEMININE |  |
| --- | --- | --- | --- |
| SING. | **quel?** | **quelle?** | *what?; which?* |
| PLUR. | **quels?** | **quelles?** | *what?; which?* |

- Interrogative adjectives agree in number and gender with the noun → 1

- The forms shown above are also used in indirect questions → 2

## ❑ Exclamatory Adjectives

|  | MASCULINE | FEMININE |  |
| --- | --- | --- | --- |
| SING. | **quel!** | **quelle!** | *what (a)!* |
| PLUR. | **quels!** | **quelles!** | *what!* |

- Exclamatory adjectives agree in number and gender with the noun → 3

- For other exclamations, see p 214.

1. **Quel genre d'homme est-ce?**
   What type of man is he?
   **Quelle est leur décision?**
   What is their decision?
   **Vous jouez de quels instruments?**
   What instruments do you play?
   **Quelles offres avez-vous reçues?**
   What offers have you received?
   **Quel vin recommandez-vous?**
   Which wine do you recommend?
   **Quelles couleurs préférez-vous?**
   Which colours do you prefer?

2. **Je ne sais pas à quelle heure il est arrivé**
   I don't know what time he arrived
   **Dites-moi quels sont les livres les plus intéressants**
   Tell me which books are the most interesting

3. **Quel dommage!**
   What a pity!
   **Quelle idée!**
   What an idea!
   **Quels beaux livres vous avez!**
   What fine books you have!
   **Quelles jolies fleurs!**
   What nice flowers!

## ◻ Possessive Adjectives

| WITH SING. NOUN | | WITH PLUR. NOUN | |
|---|---|---|---|
| MASC. | FEM. | MASC./FEM. | |
| mon | ma (mon) | mes | *my* |
| ton | ta (ton) | tes | *your* |
| son | sa (son) | ses | *his; her; its* |
| notre | notre | nos | *our* |
| votre | votre | vos | *your* |
| leur | leur | leurs | *their* |

+ Possessive adjectives agree in number and gender with the noun, NOT WITH THE OWNER → ①

+ The forms shown in brackets are used when the following word begins with a vowel or an **h** 'mute' → ②

+ **son, sa, ses** have the additional meaning of *one's* → ③

1. **Catherine a oublié son parapluie**
   Catherine has left her umbrella
   **Paul cherche sa montre**
   Paul's looking for his watch
   **Mon frère et ma sœur habitent à Glasgow**
   My brother and sister live in Glasgow
   **Est-ce que tes voisins ont vendu leur voiture?**
   Did your neighbours sell their car?
   **Rangez vos affaires**
   Put your things away

2. **mon appareil-photo**
   my camera
   **ton histoire**
   your story
   **son erreur**
   his/her mistake
   **mon autre sœur**
   my other sister

3. **perdre son équilibre**
   to lose one's balance
   **présenter ses excuses**
   to offer one's apologies

## ◻ Position of Adjectives

- French adjectives usually follow the noun → 1

- Adjectives of colour or nationality *always* follow the noun → 2

- As in English, demonstrative, possessive, numerical and interrogative adjectives precede the noun → 3

- The adjectives **autre** *other* and **chaque** *each, every* precede the noun → 4

- The following common adjectives can precede the noun:

| | | | |
|---|---|---|---|
| **beau** | *beautiful* | **jeune** | *young* |
| **bon** | *good* | **joli** | *pretty* |
| **court** | *short* | **long** | *long* |
| **dernier** | *last* | **mauvais** | *bad* |
| **grand** | *great* | **petit** | *small* |
| **gros** | *big* | **tel** | *such (a)* |
| **haut** | *high* | **vieux** | *old* |

- The meaning of the following adjectives varies according to their position:

| | BEFORE NOUN | AFTER NOUN | |
|---|---|---|---|
| **ancien** | *former* | *old, ancient* | → 5 |
| **brave** | *good* | *brave* | → 6 |
| **cher** | *dear (beloved)* | *expensive* | → 7 |
| **grand** | *great* | *tall* | → 8 |
| **même** | *same* | *very* | → 9 |
| **pauvre** | *poor (wretched)* | *poor (not rich)* | → 10 |
| **propre** | *own* | *clean* | → 11 |
| **seul** | *single, sole* | *on one's own* | → 12 |
| **simple** | *mere, simple* | *simple, easy* | → 13 |
| **vrai** | *real* | *true* | → 14 |

Adjectives following the noun are linked by **et** → 15

# Examples

| | | |
|---|---|---|
| 1 | **le chapitre suivant**<br>the following chapter | **l'heure exacte**<br>the right time |
| 2 | **une cravate rouge**<br>a red tie | **un mot français**<br>a French word |
| 3 | **ce dictionnaire**<br>this dictionary | **mon père**<br>my father |
| | **le premier étage**<br>the first floor | **deux exemples**<br>two examples |
| | **quel homme?**<br>which man? | |
| 4 | **une autre fois**<br>another time | **chaque jour**<br>every day |
| 5 | **un ancien collègue**<br>a former colleague | **l'histoire ancienne**<br>ancient history |
| 6 | **un brave homme**<br>a good man | **un homme brave**<br>a brave man |
| 7 | **mes chers amis**<br>my dear friends | **une robe chère**<br>an expensive dress |
| 8 | **un grand peintre**<br>a great painter | **un homme grand**<br>a tall man |
| 9 | **la même réponse**<br>the same answer | **vos paroles mêmes**<br>your very words |
| 10 | **cette pauvre femme**<br>that poor woman | **une nation pauvre**<br>a poor nation |
| 11 | **ma propre vie**<br>my own life | **une chemise propre**<br>a clean shirt |
| 12 | **une seule réponse**<br>a single reply | **une femme seule**<br>a woman on her own |
| 13 | **un simple regard**<br>a mere look | **un problème simple**<br>a simple problem |
| 14 | **la vraie raison**<br>the real reason | **les faits vrais**<br>the true facts |
| 15 | **un acte lâche et trompeur**<br>a cowardly, deceitful act | |
| | **un acte lâche, trompeur et ignoble**<br>a cowardly, deceitful and ignoble act | |

☐ **Personal Pronouns**

|  | SUBJECT PRONOUNS | |
|---|---|---|
| PERSON | SINGULAR | PLURAL |
| 1st | **je (j')** | **nous** |
| | *I* | *we* |
| 2nd | **tu** | **vous** |
| | *you* | *you* |
| 3rd (masc.) | **il** | **ils** |
| | *he; it* | *they* |
| (fem.) | **elle** | **elles** |
| | *she; it* | *they* |

**je** changes to **j'** before a vowel, an **h** 'mute', or the pronoun **y** →  1

• **tu/vous**

Vous, as well as being the second person plural, is also used when addressing one person. As a general rule, use **tu** only when addressing a friend, a child, a relative, someone you know very well, or when invited to do so. In all other cases use **vous**. For singular and plural uses of **vous**, see example 2

• **il/elle; ils/elles**

The form of the 3rd person pronouns reflects the number and gender of the noun(s) they replace, referring to animals and things as well as to people. **Ils** also replaces a combination of masculine and feminine nouns → 3

• Sometimes stressed pronouns replace the subject pronouns, see p 172.

1. **J'arrive!**
   I'm just coming!
   **J'en ai trois**
   I've got 3 of them
   **J'hésite à le déranger**
   I hesitate to disturb him
   **J'y pense souvent**
   I often think about it

2. Compare:    **Vous êtes certain, Monsieur Leclerc?**
                Are you sure, Mr Leclerc?
   and:        **Vous êtes certains, les enfants?**
                Are you sure, children?
   Compare:    **Vous êtes partie quand, Estelle?**
                When did you leave, Estelle?
   and:        **Estelle et Sophie – vous êtes parties quand?**
                Estelle and Sophie – when did you leave?

3. **Où logent ton père et ta mère quand ils vont à Rome?**
   Where do your father and mother stay when they go to Rome?
   **Donne-moi le journal et les lettres quand ils arriveront**
   Give me the newspaper and the letters when they arrive

## ❒ Personal Pronouns *(Continued)*

|  | DIRECT OBJECT PRONOUNS | |
|---|---|---|
| PERSON | SINGULAR | PLURAL |
| 1st | **me (m')** | **nous** |
|  | me | us |
| 2nd | **te (t')** | **vous** |
|  | you | you |
| 3rd (masc.) | **le (l')** | **les** |
|  | him; it | them |
| (fem.) | **la (l')** | **les** |
|  | her; it | them |

The forms shown in brackets are used before a vowel, an **h** 'mute', or the pronoun **y** → ①

♦ In positive commands **me** and **te** change to **moi** and **toi** except before **en** or **y** → ②

♦ **le** sometimes functions as a 'neuter' pronoun, referring to an idea or information contained in a previous statement or question. It is often not translated → ③

### Position of direct object pronouns

♦ In constructions other than the imperative affirmative the pronoun comes before the verb → ④

The same applies when the verb is in the infinitive → ⑤

In the imperative affirmative, the pronoun follows the verb and is attached to it by a hyphen → ⑥

♦ For further information, see Order of Object Pronouns, p 170.

### Reflexive Pronouns

These are dealt with under reflexive verbs, p 30.

**1**
**Il m'a vu**
He saw me
**Je ne t'oublierai jamais**
I'll never forget you
**Ça l'habitue à travailler seul**
That gets him/her used to working on his/her own
**Je veux l'y accoutumer**
I want to accustom him/her to it

**2**  **Avertis-moi de ta décision → Avertis-m'en**
Inform me of your decision     Inform me of it

**3**  **Il n'est pas là. – Je le sais bien.**
He isn't there. – I know that.
**Aidez-moi si vous le pouvez**
Help me if you can
**Elle viendra demain. – Je l'espère bien.**
She'll come tomorrow. – I hope so.

**4**  **Je t'aime**
I love you
**Les voyez-vous?**
Can you see them?
**Elle ne nous connaît pas**
She doesn't know us
**Est-ce que tu ne les aimes pas?**
Don't you like them?
**Ne me faites pas rire**
Don't make me laugh

**5**  **Puis-je vous aider?**
May I help you?

**6**  **Aidez-moi**                **Suivez-nous**
Help me                        Follow us

## ❐ Personal Pronouns *(Continued)*

|  | INDIRECT OBJECT PRONOUNS | |
|---|---|---|
| PERSON | SINGULAR | PLURAL |
| 1st | **me (m')** | **nous** |
| 2nd | **te (t')** | **vous** |
| 3rd (masc.) | **lui** | **leur** |
| (fem.) | **lui** | **leur** |

**me** and **te** change to **m'** and **t'** before a vowel or an **h** 'mute' →

- In positive commands, **me** and **te** change to **moi** and **toi** except before **en** → 2

- The pronouns shown in the above table replace the preposition **à** + noun, where the noun is a person or an animal → 3

- The verbal construction affects the translation of the pronoun → 4

### Position of indirect object pronouns

- In constructions other than the imperative affirmative, the pronoun comes before the verb → 5
  The same applies when the verb is in the infinitive → 6
  In the imperative affirmative, the pronoun follows the verb and is attached to it by a hyphen → 7

- For further information, see Order of Object Pronouns, p 170.

### Reflexive Pronouns

These are dealt with under reflexive verbs, p 30.

**1**   **Tu m'as donné ce livre**
You gave me this book
**Ils t'ont caché les faits**
They hid the facts from you

**2**   **Donnez-moi du sucre**     → **Donnez-m'en**
Give me some sugar         Give me some
**Garde-toi assez d'argent**   → **Garde-t'en assez**
Keep enough money for      Keep enough for yourself
yourself

**3**   **J'écris à Suzanne**       → **Je lui écris**
I'm writing to Suzanne      I'm writing to her
**Donne du lait au chat**    → **Donne-lui du lait**
Give the cat some milk       Give it some milk

**4**   **arracher qch à qn**        to snatch sth from sb:
         **Un voleur m'a arraché mon porte-monnaie**
         A thief snatched my purse from me
**promettre qch à qn**       to promise sb sth:
         **Il leur a promis un cadeau**
         He promised them a present
**demander à qn de faire**    to ask sb to do:
         **Elle nous avait demandé de revenir**
         She had asked us to come back

**5**   **Elle vous a écrit**        **Vous a-t-elle écrit?**
She's written to you         Has she written to you?
**Il ne nous parle pas**
He doesn't speak to us
**Est-ce que cela ne vous intéresse pas?**
Doesn't it interest you?
**Ne leur répondez pas**
Don't answer them

**6**   **Voulez-vous leur envoyer l'adresse?**
Do you want to send them the address?

**7**   **Répondez-moi**         **Donnez-nous la réponse**
Answer me            Tell us the answer

## ◻ **Personal Pronouns** *(Continued)*

### Order of object pronouns

◆ When two object pronouns of different persons come before the verb, the order is: indirect before direct, i.e.

| me te nous vous | before | le la les | → ☐1 |

◆ When two 3rd person object pronouns come before the verb, the order is: direct before indirect, i.e.

| le la les | before | lui leur | → ☐2 |

◆ When two object pronouns come after the verb (i.e. in the imperative affirmative), the order is: direct before indirect, i.e.

| le la les | before | moi toi lui nous vous leur | → ☐3 |

◆ The pronouns **y** and **en** (see pp 176 and 174) always come last → ☐4

1. **Dominique vous l'envoie demain**
   Dominique's sending it to you tomorrow
   **Est-ce qu'il te les a montrés?**
   Has he shown them to you?
   **Ne me le dis pas**
   Don't tell me (it)
   **Il ne veut pas nous la prêter**
   He won't lend it to us

2. **Elle le leur a emprunté**
   She borrowed it from them
   **Je les lui ai lus**
   I read them to him/her
   **Ne la leur donne pas**
   Don't give it to them
   **Je voudrais les lui rendre**
   I'd like to give them back to him/her

3. **Rends-les-moi**
   Give them back to me
   **Donnez-le-nous**
   Give it to us
   **Apportons-les-leur**
   Let's take them to them

4. **Donnez-leur-en**
   Give them some
   **Je l'y ai déposé**
   I dropped him there
   **Ne nous en parlez plus**
   Don't speak to us about it any more

◻ **Personal Pronouns** (Continued)

| STRESSED OR DISJUNCTIVE PRONOUNS | | |
|---|---|---|
| PERSON | SINGULAR | PLURAL |
| 1st | **moi** | **nous** |
| | *me* | *us* |
| 2nd | **toi** | **vous** |
| | *you* | *you* |
| 3rd (masc.) | **lui** | **eux** |
| | *him; it* | *them* |
| (fem.) | **elle** | **elles** |
| | *her; it* | *them* |
| ('reflexive') | **soi** | |
| | *oneself* | |

• These pronouns are used:

– after prepositions → 1
– on their own → 2
– following **c'est, ce sont** *it is* → 3
– for emphasis, especially where contrast is involved → 4
– when the subject consists of two or more pronouns → 5
– when the subject consists of a pronoun and a noun → 6
– in comparisons → 7
– before relative pronouns → 8

• For particular emphasis **-même** (singular) or **-mêmes** (plural) is
added to the pronoun → 9

| | | | |
|---|---|---|---|
| **moi-même** | *myself* | **nous-mêmes** | *ourselves* |
| **toi-même** | *yourself* | **vous-même** | *yourself* |
| **lui-même** | *himself; itself* | **vous-mêmes** | *yourselves* |
| **elle-même** | *herself; itself* | **eux-mêmes** | *themselves* |
| **soi-même** | *oneself* | **elles-mêmes** | *themselves* |

1. **Je pense à toi**
   I think about you
   **C'est pour elle**
   This is for her
   **Venez avec moi**
   Come with me

   **Partez sans eux**
   Leave without them
   **Assieds-toi à côté de lui**
   Sit beside him
   **Il a besoin de nous**
   He needs us

2. **Qui a fait cela? – Lui.**
   Who did that? – He did.
   **Qui est-ce qui gagne? – Moi**
   Who's winning? – Me

3. **C'est toi, Simon? – Non, c'est moi, David.**
   Is that you, Simon? – No, it's me, David.
   **Qui est-ce? – Ce sont eux.**
   Who is it? – It's them.

4. **Ils voyagent séparément: lui par le train, elle en autobus**
   They travel separately: he by train and she by bus
   **Toi, tu ressembles à ton père, eux pas**
   *You* look like your father, *they* don't
   **Il n'a pas l'air de s'ennuyer, lui!**
   *He* doesn't look bored!

5. **Lui et moi partons demain**
   He and I are leaving tomorrow
   **Ni vous ni elles ne pouvez rester**
   Neither you nor they can stay

6. **Mon père et elle ne s'entendent pas**
   My father and she don't get on

7. **plus jeune que moi**
   younger than me
   **Il est moins grand que toi**
   He's smaller than you (are)

8. **Moi, qui étais malade, je n'ai pas pu les accompagner**
   I, who was ill, couldn't go with them
   **Ce sont eux qui font du bruit, pas nous**
   They're the ones making the noise, not us

9. **Je l'ai fait moi-même**
   I did it myself

## ❏ The pronoun en

- **en** replaces the preposition **de** + noun → [1]
  The verbal construction can affect the translation → [2]

- **en** also replaces the partitive article *(English = some, any)* + noun → [3]

In expressions of quantity **en** represents the noun → [4]

- Position:

  **en** comes before the verb, except in positive commands when it follows and is attached to the verb by a hyphen → [5]

- **en** follows other object pronouns → [6]

---

**1** **Il est fier de son succès** → **Il en est fier**
He's proud of his success    He's proud of it
**Elle est sortie du cinéma** → **Elle en est sortie**
She came out of the cinema   She came out (of it)
**Je suis couvert de peinture** → **J'en suis couvert**
I'm covered in paint   I'm covered in it
**Il a beaucoup d'amis** → **Il en a beaucoup**
He has lots of friends   He has lots (of them)

**2** **avoir besoin de qch**   to need sth:
  **J'en ai besoin**
  I need it/them
**avoir peur de qch**   to be afraid of sth:
  **J'en ai peur**
  I'm afraid of it/them

**3** **Avez-vous de l'argent?** → **En avez-vous?**
Have you any money?   Do you have any?
**Je veux acheter des timbres** → **Je veux en acheter**
I want to buy some stamps   I want to buy some

**4** **J'ai deux crayons** → **J'en ai deux**
I've two pencils   I've two (of them)
**Combien de sœurs as-tu? – J'en ai trois.**
How many sisters do you have? – I have three.

**5** **Elle en a discuté avec moi**
She discussed it with me
**En êtes-vous content?**
Are you pleased with it/them?
**Je veux en garder trois**
I want to keep three of them
**N'en parlez plus**
Don't talk about it any more
**Prenez-en**   **Soyez-en fier**
Take some   Be proud of it/them

**6** **Donnez-leur-en**   **Il m'en a parlé**
Give them some   He spoke to me about it

## ◻ The pronoun y

- **y** replaces the preposition **à** + noun → 1
  The verbal construction can affect the translation → 2

- **y** also replaces the prepositions **dans** and **sur** + noun → 3

- **y** can also mean *there* → 4

- Position:
  **y** comes before the verb, except in positive commands when it
  follows and is attached to the verb by a hyphen → 5

- **y** follows other object pronouns → 6

| | |
|---|---|
| **1**  **Ne touchez pas à ce bouton**<br>Don't touch this switch | **→ N'y touchez pas**<br>Don't touch it |
|     **Il participe aux concerts**<br>He takes part in the concerts | **→ Il y participe**<br>He takes part (in them) |

**2**  **penser à qch**              to think about sth:
       **J'y pense souvent**
       I often think about it
    **consentir à qch**        to agree to sth:
       **Tu y as consenti?**
       Have you agreed to it?

| | |
|---|---|
| **3**  **Mettez-les dans la boîte**<br>Put them in the box | **→ Mettez-les-y**<br>Put them in it |
|     **Il les a mis sur les étagères**<br>He put them on the shelves | **→ Il les y a mis**<br>He put them on them |
|     **J'ai placé de l'argent sur ce compte**<br>I've put money into this account | **→ J'y ai placé de l'argent**<br>I've put money into it |

**4**  **Elle y passe tout l'été**
    She spends the whole summer there

**5**  **Il y a ajouté du sucre**
    He added sugar to it
    **Elle n'y a pas écrit son nom**
    She hasn't written her name on it
    **Comment fait-on pour y aller?**
    How do you get there?
    **N'y pense plus!**
    Don't give it another thought!

| | |
|---|---|
| **Restez-y**<br>Stay there | **Réfléchissez-y**<br>Think it over |

| | |
|---|---|
| **6**  **Elle m'y a conduit**<br>She drove me there | **Menez-nous-y**<br>Take us there |

## ▢ Indefinite Pronouns

| | | |
|---|---|---|
| aucun(e) | *none, not any* | → 1 |
| certain(e)s | *some, certain* | → 2 |
| chacun(e) | *each (one)* | → 3 |
| | *everybody* | |
| on | *one, you* | |
| | *somebody* | → 4 |
| | *they, people* | |
| | *we (informal use)* | |
| personne | *nobody* | → 5 |
| plusieurs | *several* | → 6 |
| quelque chose | *something; anything* | → 7 |
| quelques-un(e)s | *some, a few* | → 8 |
| quelqu'un | *somebody; anybody* | → 9 |
| rien | *nothing* | → 10 |
| tout | *all; everything* | → 11 |
| tous (toutes) | *all* | → 12 |
| l'un(e) … l'autre | *(the) one … the other* | |
| les un(e)s … les autres | *some … others* | → 13 |

◆ **aucun(e), personne, rien**

When used as subject or object of the verb, these require the word **ne** placed immediately before the verb. Note that **aucun** further needs the pronoun **en** when used as an object → 14

◆ **quelque chose, rien**

When qualified by an adjective, these pronouns require the preposition **de** before the adjective → 15

1. **Combien en avez-vous? – Aucun**
How many have you got? – None

2. **Certains pensent que …**
Some (people) think that …

3. **Chacune de ces boîtes est pleine**     **Chacun son tour!**
Each of these boxes is full     Everybody in turn!

4. **On voit l'église de cette fenêtre**
You can see the church from this window
**À la campagne on se couche tôt**
In the country they/we go to bed early
**Est-ce qu'on lui a permis de rester?**
Was he/she allowed to stay?

5. **Qui voyez-vous? – Personne**
Who can you see? – Nobody

6. **Ils sont plusieurs**
There are several of them

7. **Mange donc quelque chose!**     **Tu as vu quelque chose?**
Eat something!     Did you see anything?

8. **Je connais quelques-uns de ses amis**
I know some of his/her friends

9. **Quelqu'un a appelé**     **Tu as vu quelqu'un?**
Somebody called (out)     Did you see anybody?

10. **Qu'est-ce que tu as dans la main? – Rien**
What have you got in your hand? – Nothing

11. **Il a tout gâché**     **Tout va bien**
He has spoiled everything     All's well

12. **Tu les as tous?**     **Elles sont toutes venues**
Do you have all of them?     They all came

13. **Les uns sont satisfaits, les autres pas**
Some are satisfied, (the) others aren't

14. **Je ne vois personne**     **Rien ne lui plaît**
I can't see anyone     Nothing pleases him/her
**Aucune des entreprises ne veut …**     **Il n'en a aucun**
None of the companies wants …     He hasn't any (of them)

15. **quelque chose de grand**     **rien d'intéressant**
something big     nothing interesting

## ◻ Relative Pronouns

| | |
|---|---|
| **qui** | *who; which* |
| **que** | *who(m); which* |

These are subject and direct object pronouns that introduce a clause and refer to people or things.

| | | PEOPLE | THINGS |
|---|---|---|---|
| SUBJECT | | **qui** → 1 | **qui** → 3 |
| | | *who, that* | *which, that* |
| DIRECT | | **que (qu')** → 2 | **que (qu')** → 4 |
| OBJECT | | *who(m), that* | *which, that* |

- **que** changes to **qu'** before a vowel → 2/4

- You cannot omit the object relative pronoun in French as you can in English → 2/4

After a preposition:

- When referring to people, use **qui** → 5
  EXCEPTIONS: after **parmi** *among* and **entre** *between* use **lesquels/ lesquelles** (see below) → 6

- When referring to things, use forms of **lequel**:

| | MASCULINE | FEMININE | |
|---|---|---|---|
| SING. | **lequel** | **laquelle** | *which* |
| PLUR. | **lesquels** | **lesquelles** | *which* |

The pronoun agrees in number and gender with the noun → 7

- After the prepositions **à** and **de**, **lequel** and **lesquel(le)s** contract as follows:

  **à + lequel → auquel**
  **à + lesquels → auxquels**      → 8
  **à + lesquelles → auxquelles**

  **de + lequel → duquel**
  **de + lesquels → desquels**     → 9
  **de + lesquelles → desquelles**

1. **Mon frère, qui a vingt ans, est à l'université**
   My brother, who's twenty, is at university

2. **Les amis que je vois le plus sont ...**
   The friends (that) I see most are ...
   **Lucienne, qu'il connaît depuis longtemps, est ...**
   Lucienne, whom he has known for a long time, is ...

3. **Il y a un escalier qui mène au toit**
   There's a staircase which leads to the roof

4. **La maison que nous avons achetée a ...**
   The house (which) we've bought has ...
   **Voici le cadeau qu'elle m'a envoyé**
   This is the present (that) she sent me

5. **la personne à qui il parle**
   the person he's talking to
   **la personne avec qui je voyage**
   the person with whom I travel
   **les enfants pour qui je l'ai acheté**
   the children for whom I bought it

6. **Il y avait des jeunes, parmi lesquels Robert**
   There were some young people, Robert among them
   **les filles entre lesquelles j'étais assis**
   the girls between whom I was sitting

7. **le torchon avec lequel il l'essuie**
   the cloth he's wiping it with
   **la table sur laquelle je l'ai mis**
   the table on which I put it
   **les moyens par lesquels il l'accomplit**
   the means by which he achieves it
   **les pièces pour lesquelles elle est connue**
   the plays for which she is famous

8. **le magasin auquel il livre ces marchandises**
   the shop to which he delivers these goods

9. **les injustices desquelles il se plaint**
   the injustices he's complaining about

## ❑ Relative Pronouns (Continued)

**quoi**   which, what

◆ When the relative pronoun does not refer to a specific noun, **quoi** is
  used after a preposition → ①

**dont**   whose, of whom, of which

◆ **dont** often (but not always) replaces **de qui**, **duquel**, **de laquelle**,
  and **desquel(le)s** → ②

◆ It cannot replace **de qui**, **duquel** *etc* in the construction preposition
  + noun + **de qui/duquel** → ③

1.  **C'est en quoi vous vous trompez**
    That's where you're wrong
    **À quoi, j'ai répondu '…'**
    To which I replied, '…'

2.  **la femme dont (= de qui) la voiture est garée en face**
    the woman whose car is parked opposite
    **un prix dont (= de qui) je suis fier**
    an award I am proud of
    **un ami dont (= de qui) je connais le frère**
    a friend whose brother I know
    **les enfants dont (= de qui) vous vous occupez**
    the children you look after
    **le film dont (= duquel) il a parlé**
    the film of which he spoke
    **la fenêtre dont (= de laquelle) les rideaux sont tirés**
    the window whose curtains are drawn
    **des livres dont (= desquels) j'ai oublié les titres**
    books whose titles I've forgotten
    **les maladies dont (= desquelles) il souffre**
    the illnesses he suffers from

3.  **une personne sur l'aide de qui on peut compter**
    a person whose help one can rely on
    **les enfants aux parents de qui j'écris**
    the children to whose parents I'm writing
    **la maison dans le jardin de laquelle il y a …**
    the house in whose garden there is …

❏ **Relative Pronouns** (Continued)

**ce qui, ce que**     *that which, what*

These are used when the relative pronoun does not refer to a specific noun, and they are often translated as *what* (literally: *that which*)

    **ce qui**         is used as the subject → 1
    **ce que\***      is used as the direct object → 2

    **\*que** changes to **qu'** before a vowel → 2

- Note the construction

    **tout ce qui**     ⎫
    **tout ce que**    ⎬     *everything/all that* → 3

- **de + ce que → ce dont** → 4

- preposition + **ce que → ce** + preposition + **quoi** → 5

- When **ce qui, ce que** *etc*, refers to a previous CLAUSE the translation is *which* → 6

1. **Ce qui m'intéresse ne l'intéresse pas forcément**
   What interests me doesn't necessarily interest him
   **Je n'ai pas vu ce qui s'est passé**
   I didn't see what happened

2. **Ce que j'aime c'est la musique classique**
   What I like is classical music
   **Montrez-moi ce qu'il vous a donné**
   Show me what he gave you

3. **Tout ce qui reste c'est …**
   All that's left is …
   **Donnez-moi tout ce que vous avez**
   Give me everything you have

4. **Il risque de perdre ce dont il est si fier**
   He risks losing what he's so proud of
   **Voilà ce dont il s'agit**
   That's what it's about

5. **Ce n'est pas ce à quoi je m'attendais**
   It's not what I was expecting
   **Ce à quoi je m'intéresse particulièrement c'est …**
   What I'm particularly interested in is …

6. **Il est d'accord, ce qui m'étonne**
   He agrees, which surprises me
   **Il a dit qu'elle ne venait pas, ce que nous savions déjà**
   He said she wasn't coming, which we already knew

## ❑ Interrogative Pronouns

| | |
|---|---|
| **qui?** | who; whom? |
| **que?** | what? |
| **quoi?** | what? |

These pronouns are used in direct questions.

The form of the pronoun depends on:
- whether it refers to people or to things
- whether it is the subject or object of the verb, or if it comes after a preposition

**Qui** and **que** have longer forms, as shown in the tables below.

♦ Referring to people:

| | | |
|---|---|---|
| SUBJECT | **qui?** | |
| | **qui est-ce qui?** | → ① |
| | *who?* | |
| OBJECT | **qui?** | |
| | **qui est-ce que\*?** | → ② |
| | *who(m)?* | |
| AFTER PREPOSITIONS | **qui?** | → ③ |
| | *who(m)?* | |

♦ Referring to things:

| | | |
|---|---|---|
| SUBJECT | **qu'est-ce qui?** | → ④ |
| | *what?* | |
| OBJECT | **que\*?** | |
| | **qu'est-ce que\*?** | → ⑤ |
| | *what?* | |
| AFTER PREPOSITIONS | **quoi?** | → ⑥ |
| | *what?* | |

**\*que** changes to **qu'** before a vowel → ②, ⑤

Grammar

1. **Qui vient?**
   **Qui est-ce qui vient?**
   Who's coming?

2. **Qui vois-tu?**
   **Qui est-ce que tu vois?**
   Who(m) can you see?
   **Qui a-t-elle rencontré?**
   **Qui est-ce qu'elle a rencontré?**
   Who(m) did she meet?

3. **De qui parle-t-il?**
   Who's he talking about?
   **Pour qui est ce livre?**
   Who's this book for?
   **À qui avez-vous écrit?**
   To whom did you write?

4. **Qu'est-ce qui se passe?**
   What's happening?
   **Qu'est-ce qui a vexé Paul?**
   What upset Paul?

5. **Que faites-vous?**
   **Qu'est-ce que vous faites?**
   What are you doing?
   **Qu'a-t-il dit?**
   **Qu'est-ce qu'il a dit?**
   What did he say?

6. **À quoi cela sert-il?**
   What's that used for?
   **De quoi a-t-on parlé?**
   What was the discussion about?
   **Sur quoi vous basez-vous?**
   What do you base it on?

## □ Interrogative Pronouns (Continued)

| | |
|---|---|
| **qui** | who; whom |
| **ce qui** | what |
| **ce que** | what |
| **quoi** | what |

These pronouns are used in indirect questions.
The form of the pronoun depends on:
  – whether it refers to people or to things
  – whether it is the subject or object of the verb, or if it comes after
    a preposition

◆ Referring to people: use **qui** in all instances → ①

◆ Referring to things:

| SUBJECT | **ce qui** | → ② |
|---|---|---|
| | *what* | |
| OBJECT | **ce que*** | → ③ |
| | *what* | |
| AFTER | **quoi** | → ④ |
| PREPOSITIONS | *what* | |

***que** changes to **qu'** before a vowel → ③

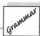

① **Demande-lui qui est venu**
Ask him who came
**Je me demande qui ils ont vu**
I wonder who they saw
**Dites-moi qui vous préférez**
Tell me who you prefer
**Elle ne sait pas à qui s'adresser**
She doesn't know who to apply to
**Demandez-leur pour qui elles travaillent**
Ask them who they work for

② **Il se demande ce qui se passe**
He's wondering what's happening
**Je ne sais pas ce qui vous fait croire que ...**
I don't know what makes you think that ...

③ **Raconte-nous ce que tu as fait**
Tell us what you did
**Je me demande ce qu'elle pense**
I wonder what she's thinking

④ **On ne sait pas de quoi vivent ces animaux**
We don't know what these animals live on
**Je vais lui demander à quoi il fait allusion**
I'm going to ask him what he's hinting at

❒ **Interrogative Pronouns** *(Continued)*

**lequel?, laquelle?; lesquels?, lesquelles?**

|  | MASCULINE | FEMININE |  |
|---|---|---|---|
| SING. | **lequel?** | **laquelle?** | *which (one)?* |
| PLUR. | **lesquels?** | **lesquelles?** | *which (ones)?* |

♦ The pronoun agrees in number and gender with the noun it refers to → ☐1

♦ The same forms are used in indirect questions → ☐2

♦ After the prepositions **à** and **de**, **lequel** and **lesquel(le)s** contract as follows:

**à + lequel? → auquel?**
**à + lesquels? → auxquels?**
**à + lesquelles? → auxquelles?**

**de + lequel? → duquel?**
**de + lesquels? → desquels?**
**de + lesquelles? → desquelles?**

# Examples

1 **J'ai choisi un livre. – Lequel?**
I've chosen a book. – Which one?
**Laquelle de ces valises est la vôtre?**
Which of these cases is yours?
**Amenez quelques amis. – Lesquels?**
Bring some friends. – Which ones?
**Lesquelles de vos sœurs sont mariées?**
Which of your sisters are married?

2 **Je me demande laquelle des maisons est la leur**
I wonder which is their house
**Dites-moi lesquels d'entre eux étaient là**
Tell me which of them were there

## ❏ Possessive Pronouns

| SINGULAR | | |
|---|---|---|
| MASCULINE | FEMININE | |
| le mien | la mienne | *mine* |
| le tien | la tienne | *yours* |
| le sien | la sienne | *his; hers; its* |
| le nôtre | la nôtre | *ours* |
| le vôtre | la vôtre | *yours* |
| le leur | la leur | *theirs* |

| PLURAL | | |
|---|---|---|
| MASCULINE | FEMININE | |
| les miens | les miennes | *mine* |
| les tiens | les tiennes | *yours* |
| les siens | les siennes | *his; hers; its* |
| les nôtres | les nôtres | *ours* |
| les vôtres | les vôtres | *yours* |
| les leurs | les leurs | *theirs* |

* The pronoun agrees in number and gender with the noun it replaces, NOT WITH THE OWNER → ①

* Alternative translations are *my own, your own* etc; **le sien, la sienne** etc may also mean *one's own* → ②

* After the prepositions **à** and **de** the articles **le** and **les** are contracted in the normal way (see p 140):

à + le mien → au mien
à + les miens → aux miens                → ③
à + les miennes → aux miennes

de + le mien → du mien
de + les miens → des miens               → ④
de + les miennes → des miennes

① **Demandez à Carole si ce stylo est le sien**
Ask Carole if this pen is hers
**Quelle équipe a gagné – la leur ou la nôtre?**
Which team won – theirs or ours?
**Mon stylo marche mieux que le tien**
My pen writes better than yours
**Richard a pris mes affaires pour les siennes**
Richard mistook my belongings for his
**Si tu n'as pas de disques, emprunte les miens**
If you don't have any records, borrow mine
**Nos maisons sont moins grandes que les vôtres**
Our houses are smaller than yours

② **Est-ce que leur entreprise est aussi grande que la vôtre?**
Is their company as big as your own?
**Leurs prix sont moins élevés que les nôtres**
Their prices are lower than our own
**Le bonheur des autres importe plus que le sien**
Other people's happiness matters more than one's own

③ **Pourquoi préfères-tu ce manteau au mien?**
Why do you prefer this coat to mine?
**Quelles maisons ressemblent aux leurs?**
Which houses resemble theirs?

④ **Leur car est garé**
Their coach is parked
**Vos livres sont au-dessus des miens**
Your books are on top of mine

## ☐ Demonstrative Pronouns

**celui, celle; ceux, celles**

|        | MASCULINE | FEMININE |          |
|--------|-----------|----------|----------|
| SING.  | **celui** | **celle**  | *the one* |
| PLUR.  | **ceux**  | **celles** | *the ones* |

* The pronoun agrees in number and gender with the noun it replaces
  → 1

* Uses:

  – preceding a relative pronoun, meaning *the one(s) who/which* → 1
  – preceding the preposition **de**, meaning *the one(s) belonging to, the one(s) of* → 2
  – with **-ci** and **-là**, for emphasis or to distinguish between two things:

|        | MASCULINE   | FEMININE    |                |       |
|--------|-------------|-------------|----------------|-------|
| SING.  | **celui-ci** | **celle-ci** | *this (one)*    | → 3  |
| PLUR.  | **ceux-ci**  | **celles-ci** | *these (ones)* |       |

|        | MASCULINE   | FEMININE    |                |       |
|--------|-------------|-------------|----------------|-------|
| SING.  | **celui-là** | **celle-là** | *that(one)*     | → 3  |
| PLUR.  | **ceux-là**  | **celles-là** | *those (ones)* |       |

  – an additional meaning of **celui-ci/celui-là** *etc* is *the former/the latter*.

1. **Lequel? – Celui qui parle à Anne**
   Which man? – The one who's talking to Anne
   **Quelle robe désirez-vous? – Celle qui est en vitrine**
   Which dress do you want? – The one which is in the window
   **Est-ce que ces livres sont ceux qu'il t'a donnés?**
   Are these the books that he gave you?
   **Quelles filles? – Celles que nous avons vues hier**
   Which girls? – The ones we saw yesterday
   **Cet article n'est pas celui dont vous m'avez parlé**
   This article isn't the one you spoke to me about

2. **Ce jardin est plus grand que celui de mes parents**
   This garden is bigger than my parents' (garden)
   **Est-ce que ta fille est plus âgée que celle de Gabrielle?**
   Is your daughter older than Gabrielle's (daughter)?
   **Je préfère les enfants de Paul à ceux de Roger**
   I prefer Paul's children to Roger's (children)
   **Comparez vos réponses à celles de votre voisin**
   Compare your answers with your neighbour's (answers)
   **les montagnes d'Écosse et celles du pays de Galles**
   the mountains of Scotland and those of Wales

3. **Quel tailleur préférez-vous: celui-ci ou celui-là?**
   Which suit do you prefer: this one or that one?
   **Cette chemise a deux poches mais celle-là n'en a pas**
   This shirt has two pockets but that one has none
   **Quels œufs choisirais-tu: ceux-ci ou ceux-là?**
   Which eggs would you choose: these (ones) or those (ones)?
   **De toutes mes jupes, celle-ci me va le mieux**
   Of all my skirts, this one fits me best

❐ **Demonstrative Pronouns** *(Continued)*

**ce (c')**                          *it, that*

+ Usually used with **être**, in the expressions **c'est, c'était, ce sont** *etc*
  → 1

+ Note the spelling **ç** when followed by the letter **a** → 2

+ Uses:
  – to identify a person or object → 3
  – for emphasis → 4
  – as a neuter pronoun, referring to a statement, idea *etc* → 5

**ce qui, ce que, ce dont** etc: see Relative Pronouns (p 184), Interrogative Pronouns (p 188).

**cela, ça**                          *it, that*

+ **cela** and **ça** are used as 'neuter' pronouns, referring to a statement, an idea, an object → 6

+ In everyday spoken language **ça** is used in preference to **cela**

**ceci**                          *this* → 7

+ **ceci** is not used as often as 'this' in English; **cela, ça** are often used where we use 'this'.

1. **C'est …**
It's/That's …

 **C'était moi**
It was me

2. **Ç'a été la cause de …**
It has been the cause of…

3. **Qui est-ce?**
Who is it?; Who's this/that?; Who's he/she?

 **C'est lui/mon frère/nous**
It's/That's him/my brother/us

 **Ce sont eux**
It's them

 **C'est une infirmière\***
She's a nurse

 **Ce sont des professeurs\***
They're teachers

 **Qu'est-ce que c'est?**
What's this/that?

 **Qu'est-ce que c'est que ça?**
What's that?

 **C'est une agrafeuse**
It's a stapler

 **Ce sont des trombones**
They're paper clips

4. **C'est moi qui ai téléphoné**
It was me who phoned

 **Ce sont les enfants qui importent le plus**
It's the children who matter most

5. **C'est très intéressant**
That's/It's very interesting

 **Ce serait dangereux**
That/It would be dangerous

6. **Ça ne fait rien**
It doesn't matter

 **À quoi bon faire ça?**
What's the use of doing that?

 **Cela ne compte pas**
That doesn't count

 **Cela demande du temps**
It/That takes time

7. **À qui est ceci?**
Whose is this?

 **Ouvrez-le comme ceci**
Open it like this

\*See pp 146 and 147 for the use of the article when stating a person's profession

## ❏ Adverbs

### Formation

- Most adverbs are formed by adding **-ment** to the feminine form of the adjective → 1

- **-ment** is added to the *masculine* form when the masculine form ends in **-é**, **-i** or **-u** → 2

  EXCEPTION: **gai** → 3

  Occasionally the **u** changes to **û** before **-ment** is added → 4

- If the adjective ends in **-ant** or **-ent**, the adverb ends in **-amment** or **-emment** → 5

  EXCEPTIONS: **lent, présent** → 6

### Irregular Adverbs

| ADJECTIVE | | ADVERB | | |
|---|---|---|---|---|
| **aveugle** | *blind* | **aveuglément** | blindly | |
| **bon** | *good* | **bien** | well | → 7 |
| **bref** | *brief* | **brièvement** | briefly | |
| **énorme** | *enormous* | **énormément** | enormously | |
| **exprès** | *express* | **expressément** | expressly | → 8 |
| **gentil** | *kind* | **gentiment** | kindly | |
| **mauvais** | *bad* | **mal** | badly | → 9 |
| **meilleur** | *better* | **mieux** | better | |
| **pire** | *worse* | **pis** | worse | |
| **précis** | *precise* | **précisément** | precisely | |
| **profond** | *deep* | **profondément** | deeply | → 10 |
| **traître** | *treacherous* | **traîtreusement** | treacherously | |

### Adjectives used as adverbs

Certain adjectives are used adverbially. These include: **bas, bon, cher, clair, court, doux, droit, dur, faux, ferme, fort, haut, mauvais** and **net** → 11

Grammar

1. MASC./FEM. ADJECTIVE
**heureux/heureuse** fortunate
**franc/franche** frank
**extrême/extrême** extreme

   ADVERB
**heureusement** fortunately
**franchement** frankly
**extrêmement** extremely

2. MASC. ADJECTIVE
**désespéré** desperate
**vrai** true
**résolu** resolute

   ADVERB
**désespérément** desperately
**vraiment** truly
**résolument** resolutely

3. **gai** cheerful

   **gaiement** OR **gaîment** cheerfully

4. **continu** continuous
   **continûment** continuously

5. **constant** constant
**courant** fluent
**évident** obvious
**fréquent** frequent

   **constamment** constantly
**couramment** fluently
**évidemment** obviously
**fréquemment** frequently

6. **lent** slow
**présent** present

   **lentement** slowly
**présentement** presently

7. **Elle travaille bien**
She works well

8. **Il a expressément défendu qu'on parte**
He has expressly forbidden us to leave

9. **Un emploi mal payé**
A badly paid job

10. **J'ai été profondément ému**
I was deeply moved

11. **parler bas/haut**
to speak softly/loudly
**coûter cher**
to be expensive
**voir clair**
to see clearly
**travailler dur**
to work hard
**chanter faux**
to sing off key
**sentir bon/mauvais**
to smell nice/horrible

## ◻ Position of Adverbs

◆ When the adverb accompanies a verb in a simple tense, it generally
  follows the verb → 1

◆ When the adverb accompanies a verb in a compound tense, it generally
  comes between the auxiliary verb and the past participle → 2

  Some adverbs, however, follow the past participle → 3

◆ When the adverb accompanies an adjective or another adverb it
  generally precedes the adjective/adverb → 4

## ◻ Comparatives of Adverbs

These are formed using the following constructions:

| | | |
|---|---|---|
| **plus ... (que)** | *more ... (than)* | → 5 |
| **moins ... (que)** | *less ... (than)* | → 6 |
| **aussi ... que** | *as ... as* | → 7 |
| **si ... que\*** | *as ... as* | → 8 |

\*used mainly after a negative

## ◻ Superlatives of Adverbs

These are formed using the following constructions:

| | | |
|---|---|---|
| **le plus ... (que)** | *the most ... (that)* | → 9 |
| **le moins ... (que)** | *the least ... (that)* | → 10 |

### Adverbs with irregular comparatives/superlatives

| ADVERB | COMPARATIVE | SUPERLATIVE |
|---|---|---|
| **beaucoup** | **plus** | **le plus** |
| *a lot* | *more* | *(the) most* |
| **bien** | **mieux** | **le mieux** |
| *well* | *better* | *(the) best* |
| **mal** | **pis** OR **plus mal** | **le pis** OR **le plus mal** |
| *badly* | *worse* | *(the) worst* |
| **peu** | **moins** | **le moins** |
| *little* | *less* | *(the) least* |

*Grammar*

1. **Il dort encore**
He's still asleep

   **Je pense souvent à toi**
   I often think about you

2. **Ils sont déjà partis**
They've already gone

   **J'ai presque fini**
   I'm almost finished

   **J'ai toujours cru que …**
   I've always thought that …

   **Il a trop mangé**
   He's eaten too much

3. **On les a vus partout**
We saw them everywhere

   **Elle est revenue hier**
   She came back yesterday

4. **un très beau chemisier**
a very nice blouse

   **beaucoup plus vite**
   much faster

   **une femme bien habillée**
   a well-dressed woman

   **peu souvent**
   not very often

5. **plus vite**
more quickly

   **Elle chante plus fort que moi**
   She sings louder than I do

   **plus régulièrement**
   more regularly

6. **moins facilement**
less easily

   **moins souvent**
   less often

   **Nous nous voyons moins fréquemment qu'auparavant**
   We see each other less frequently than before

7. **Faites-le aussi vite que possible**
Do it as quickly as possible

   **Il en sait aussi long que nous**
   He knows as much about it as we do

8. **Ce n'est pas si loin que je pensais**
It's not as far as I thought

9. **Marianne court le plus vite**
Marianne runs fastest

   **Le plus tôt que je puisse venir c'est samedi**
   The earliest that I can come is Saturday

10. **C'est l'auteur que je connais le moins bien**
It's the writer I'm least familiar with

## ❑ Common adverbs and their usage

| | | |
|---|---|---|
| assez | *enough; quite* | → 1 See also below |
| aussi | *also, too; as* | → 2 |
| autant | *as much* | → 3 See also below |
| beaucoup | *a lot; much* | → 4 See also below |
| bien | *well; very* | → 5 See also below |
| | *very much; 'indeed'* | |
| combien | *how much; how many* | → 6 See also below |
| comme | *how; what* | → 7 |
| déjà | *already; before* | → 8 |
| encore | *still; yet* | → 9 |
| | *more; even* | |
| moins | *less* | → 10 See also below |
| peu | *little, not much; not very* | → 11 See also below |
| plus | *more* | → 12 See also below |
| si | *so; such* | → 13 |
| tant | *so much* | → 14 See also below |
| toujours | *always; still* | → 15 |
| trop | *too much; too* | → 16 See also below |

• **assez, autant, beaucoup, combien** *etc* are used in the construction adverb + **de** + noun with the following meanings:

| | | |
|---|---|---|
| assez de | *enough* | → 17 |
| autant de | *as much; as many* | |
| | *so much; so many* | |
| beaucoup de | *a lot of* | |
| combien de | *how much; how many* | |
| moins de | *less; fewer* | → 17 |
| peu de | *little, not much; few, not many* | |
| plus de | *more* | |
| tant de | *so much; so many* | |
| trop de | *too much; too many* | |

• **bien** can be followed by a partitive article (see p 144) plus a noun to mean *a lot of; a good many* → 18

| | | |
|---|---|---|
| 1 | **Avez-vous assez chaud?** | **Il est assez tard** |
| | Are you warm enough? | It's quite late |
| 2 | **Je préfère ça aussi** | **Elle est aussi grande que moi** |
| | I prefer it too | She is as tall as I am |
| 3 | **Je voyage autant que lui** | I travel as much as him |
| | Do you read a lot? | **C'est beaucoup plus loin?** |
| 4 | **Tu lis beaucoup?** | Is it much further? |
| 5 | **Bien joué!** | **Je suis bien content que ...** |
| | Well played! | I'm very pleased that ... |
| | **Il s'est bien amusé** | **Je l'ai bien fait** |
| | He enjoyed himself very much | I DID do it |
| 6 | **Combien coûte ce livre?** | **Vous êtes combien?** |
| | How much is this book? | How many of you are there? |
| 7 | **Comme tu es jolie!** | **Comme il fait beau!** |
| | How pretty you look! | What lovely weather! |
| 8 | **Je l'ai déjà fait** | **Êtes-vous déjà allé en France?** |
| | I've already done it | Have you been to France before? |
| 9 | **J'en ai encore deux** | **Elle n'est pas encore là** |
| | I've still got two | She isn't there yet |
| | **Encore du café, Alain?** | **Encore mieux!** |
| | More coffee, Alan? | Even better! |
| 10 | **Travaillez moins** | **Je suis moins étonné que toi** |
| | Work less | I'm less surprised than you are |
| 11 | **Elle mange peu** | **C'est peu important** |
| | She doesn't eat very much | It's not very important |
| 12 | **Il se détend plus** | **Elle est plus timide que Sophie** |
| | He relaxes more | She is shyer than Sophie |
| 13 | **Simon est si charmant** | **une si belle vue** |
| | Simon is so charming | such a lovely view |
| 14 | **Elle l'aime tant** | She loves him so much |
| 15 | **Il dit toujours ça!** | **Tu le vois toujours?** |
| | He always says that! | Do you still see him? |
| 16 | **J'ai trop mangé** | **C'est trop cher** |
| | I've eaten too much | It's too expensive |
| 17 | **assez d'argent/de livres** | **moins de temps/d'amis** |
| | enough money/books | less time/fewer friends |
| 18 | **bien du mal/des gens** | a lot of harm/a good many people |

grammar

On the following pages you will find some of the most frequent uses of prepositions in French. Particular attention is paid to cases where usage differs markedly from English. It is often difficult to give an English equivalent for French prepositions, since usage *does* vary so much between the two languages.

In the list below, the broad meaning of the preposition is given on the left, with examples of usage following.

Prepositions are dealt with in alphabetical order, except **à**, **de** and **en** which are shown first.

**à**

| | | |
|---|---|---|
| *at* | **lancer qch à qn** | *to throw sth at sb* |
| | **il habite à St. Pierre** | *he lives at St. Pierre* |
| | **à 5 francs (la) pièce** | *(at) 5 francs each* |
| | **à 100 km à l'heure** | *at 100 km per hour* |
| *in* | **à la campagne** | *in the country* |
| | **à Londres** | *in London* |
| | **au lit** | *in bed (also to bed)* |
| | **un livre à la main** | *with a book in his/her hand* |
| *on* | **un tableau au mur** | *a picture on the wall* |
| *to* | **aller au cinéma** | *to go to the cinema* |
| | **donner qch à qn** | *to give sth to sb* |
| | **le premier/dernier à faire** | *the first/last to do* |
| | **demander qch à qn** | *to ask sb sth* |
| *from* | **arracher qch à qn** | *to snatch sth from sb* |
| | **acheter qch à qn** | *to buy sth from sb* |
| | **cacher qch à qn** | *to hide sth from sb* |
| | **emprunter qch à qn** | *to borrow sth from sb* |
| | **prendre qch à qn** | *to take sth from sb* |
| | **voler qch à qn** | *to steal sth from sb* |

| descriptive | **la femme au chapeau vert** | *the woman with the green hat* |
| | **un garçon aux yeux bleus** | *a boy with blue eyes* |
| manner, means | **à l'anglaise** | *in the English manner* |
| | **fait à la main** | *handmade* |
| | **à bicyclette/cheval** | *by bicycle/on horseback* (BUT note other forms of transport used with **en** and **par**) |
| | **à pied** | *on foot* |
| | **chauffer au gaz** | *to heat with/by gas* |
| | **à pas lents** | *with slow steps* |
| | **cuisiner au beurre** | *to cook with butter* |
| time, date: at, in | **à minuit** | *at midnight* |
| | **à trois heures cinq** | *at five past three* |
| | **au 20ème siècle** | *in the 20th century* |
| | **à Noël/Pâques** | *at Christmas/Easter* |
| distance | **à 6 km d'ici** | *(at a distance of) 6 km from here* |
| | **à deux pas de chez moi** | *just a step from my place* |
| destined for | **une tasse à thé** | *a teacup (compare* **une tasse de thé**, *p 206)* |
| | **un service à café** | *a coffee service* |
| after certain adjectives | **son écriture est difficile à lire** | *his writing is difficult to read (compare the usage with* **de**, *p 206)* |
| | **prêt à tout** | *ready for anything* |
| after certain verbs | see p 64 | |

**de**

| | | |
|---|---|---|
| *from* | **venir de Londres** | *to come from London* |
| | **du matin au soir** | *from morning till night* |
| | **du 21 juin au 5 juillet** | *from 21st June till 5th July* |
| | **de 10 à 15** | *from 10 to 15* |
| belonging to, *of* | **un ami de la famille** | *a family friend* |
| | **les vents d'automne** | *the autumn winds* |
| contents, composition, material | **une boîte d'allumettes** | *a box of matches* |
| | **une tasse de thé** | *a cup of tea* (compare **une tasse à thé**, p 205) |
| | **une robe de soie** | *a silk dress* |
| manner | **d'une façon irrégulière** | *in an irregular way* |
| | **d'un coup de couteau** | *with the blow of a knife* |
| quality | **la société de consommation** | *the consumer society* |
| | **des objets de valeur** | *valuable items* |
| comparative + a number | **il y avait plus/moins de cent personnes** | *there were more/fewer than a hundred people* |
| after superlatives: *in* | **la plus/moins belle ville du monde** | *the most/least beautiful city in the world* |
| after certain adjectives | **surpris de voir** | *surprised to see* |
| | **il est difficile d'y accéder** | *access is difficult* (compare the usage with **à**, p 205) |
| after certain verbs | see p 64 | |

**en**

| place: *to, in, on* | **en ville**<br>**en pleine mer**<br>**en France** | *in/to town*<br>*on the open sea*<br>*in/to France* (note that masculine countries use **à**) |
|---|---|---|
| dates, months: *in* | **en 1923**<br>**en janvier** | *in 1923*<br>*in January* |
| transport | **en voiture**<br>**en avion** | *by car*<br>*by plane* (but note usage of **à** and **par** in other expressions) |
| language | **en français** | *in French* |
| duration | **je le ferai en trois jours** | *I'll do it in three days* (i.e. *I'll take 3 days to do it:* compare **dans trois jours**, p 208) |
| material | **un bracelet en or** | *a bracelet made of gold* (note that the use of **en** stresses the material more than the use of **de**) |
| | **consister en** | *to consist of* |
| in the manner of, like a | **parler en vrai connaisseur**<br>**déguisé en cowboy** | *to speak like a real connoisseur*<br>*dressed up as a cowboy* |
| + present participle | **il l'a vu en passant devant la porte** | *he saw it as he came past the door* |

### avant

| | | |
|---|---|---|
| *before* | **il est arrivé avant toi** | *he arrived before you* |
| + infinitive (add **de**) | **je vais finir ça avant de manger** | *I'm going to finish this before eating* |
| preference | **la santé avant tout** | *health above all things* |

### chez

| | | |
|---|---|---|
| *at the home of* | **chez lui/moi** | *at his/my house* |
| | **être chez soi** | *to be at home* |
| | **venez chez nous** | *come round to our place* |
| *at/to a shop* | **chez le boucher** | *at/to the butcher's* |
| *in a person, among a group of people or animals* | **ce que je n'aime pas chez lui c'est son ...** | *what I don't like in him is his ...* |
| | **chez les fourmis** | *among ants* |

### dans

| | | |
|---|---|---|
| position | **dans une boîte** | *in(to) a box* |
| circumstance | **dans son enfance** | *in his childhood* |
| future time | **dans trois jours** | *in three days' time (compare **en trois jours**, p 207)* |

### depuis

| | | |
|---|---|---|
| *since:* time | **depuis mardi** | *since Tuesday* |
| place | **il pleut depuis Paris** | *it's been raining since Paris* |
| *for* | **il habite cette maison depuis 3 ans** | *he's been living in this house for 3 years (NOTE TENSE)* |

*grammar*

**dès**

| | | |
|---|---|---|
| past time | **dès mon enfance** | *since my childhood* |
| future time | **je le ferai dès mon retour** | *I'll do it as soon as I get back* |

**entre**

| | | |
|---|---|---|
| *between* | **entre 8 et 10** | *between 8 and 10* |
| *among* | **Jean et Pierre, entre autres** | *Jean and Pierre, among others* |
| reciprocal | **s'aider entre eux** | *to help each other (out)* |

**d'entre**

| | | |
|---|---|---|
| *of, among* | **trois d'entre eux** | *three of them* |

**par**

| | | |
|---|---|---|
| agent of passive: *by* | **renversé par une voiture** | *knocked down by a car* |
| | **tué par la foudre** | *killed by lightning* |
| weather conditions | **par un beau jour d'été** | *on a lovely summer's day* |
| *by (means of)* | **par un couloir/sentier** | *by a corridor/path* |
| | **par le train** | *by train (but see also à and en)* |
| | **par l'intermédiaire de M. Duval** | *through Mr Duval* |
| distribution | **deux par deux** | *two by two* |
| | **par groupes de dix** | *in groups of ten* |
| | **deux fois par jour** | *twice a day* |

**pour**

| | | |
|---|---|---|
| *for* | c'est pour vous | *it's for you* |
| | c'est pour demain | *it's for tomorrow* |
| | une chambre pour 2 nuits | *a room for 2 nights* |
| | pour un enfant, il se débrouille bien | *for a child he manages very well* |
| | il part pour l'Espagne | *he's leaving for Spain* |
| | il l'a fait pour vous | *he did it for you* |
| | il lui a donné 50 francs pour ce livre | *he gave him 50 francs for this book* |
| | je ne suis pas pour cette idée | *I'm not for that idea* |
| | pour qui me prends-tu? | *who do you take me for?* |
| | il passe pour un idiot | *he's taken for a fool* |
| + infinitive: *(in order) to* | elle se pencha pour le ramasser | *she bent down to pick it up* |
| | c'est trop fragile pour servir de siège | *it's too fragile to be used as a seat* |
| *to(wards)* | être bon/gentil pour qn | *to be kind to sb* |
| with prices, time | pour 200 francs d'essence | *200 francs' worth of petrol* |
| | j'en ai encore pour une heure | *I'll be another hour (at it) yet* |

**sans**

| | | |
|---|---|---|
| *without* | sans eau | *without water* |
| | sans ma femme | *without my wife* |
| + infinitive | sans compter les autres | *without counting the others* |

**sauf**

| | | |
|---|---|---|
| *except (for)* | **tous sauf lui** | *all except him* |
| | **sauf quand il pleut** | *except when it's raining* |
| *barring* | **sauf imprévu** | *barring the unexpected* |
| | **sauf avis contraire** | *unless you hear to the contrary* |

**sur**

| | | |
|---|---|---|
| *on* | **sur le siège** | *on the seat* |
| | **sur l'armoire** | *on top of the wardrobe* |
| | **sur le mur** | *on (top of) the wall (if the meaning is hanging on the wall use **à**, p 204)* |
| | **sur votre gauche** | *on your left* |
| | **être sur le point de faire** | *to be on the point of doing* |
| *on (to)* | **mettez-le sur la table** | *put it on the table* |
| *proportion: out of, by* | **8 sur 10** | *8 out of 10* |
| | **un automobiliste sur 5** | *one motorist in 5* |
| | **la pièce fait 2 mètres sur 3** | *the room measures 2 metres by 3* |

## ❒ Conjunctions

There are conjunctions which introduce a main clause, such as **et** *and*, **mais** *but*, **si** *if*, **ou** *or* etc, and those which introduce subordinate clauses like **parce que** *because*, **pendant que** *while*, **après que** *after* etc. They are all used in much the same way as in English, but the following points are of note:

♦ Some conjunctions in French require a following subjunctive, see p 58

♦ Some conjunctions are 'split' in French like *both ... and, either ... or* in English:

| | | |
|---|---|---|
| **et ... et** | *both ... and* | → 1 |
| **ni ... ni ... ne** | *neither ... nor* | → 2 |
| **ou (bien) ... ou (bien)** | *either ... or (else)* | → 3 |
| **soit ... soit** | *either ... or* | → 4 |

♦ **si + il(s)** → **s'il(s)** → 5

♦ **que**
  – meaning *that* → 6
  – replacing another conjunction → 7
  – replacing **si**, see p 62
  – in comparisons, meaning *as, than* → 8
  – followed by the subjunctive, see p 62

♦ **aussi** *so, therefore*: the subject and verb are inverted if the subject is a pronoun → 9

1. **Ces fleurs poussent et en été et en hiver**
   These flowers grow in both summer and winter

2. **Ni lui ni elle ne sont venus**
   Neither he nor she came
   **Ils n'ont ni argent ni nourriture**
   They have neither money nor food

3. **Elle doit être ou naïve ou stupide**
   She must be either naïve or stupid
   **Ou bien il m'évite ou bien il ne me reconnaît pas**
   Either he's avoiding me or else he doesn't recognize me

4. **Il faut choisir soit l'un soit l'autre**
   You have to choose either one or the other

5. **Je ne sais pas s'il vient/s'ils viennent**
   I don't know if he's coming/if they're coming
   **Dis-moi s'il y a des erreurs**
   Tell me if there are any mistakes
   **Votre passeport, s'il vous plaît**
   Your passport, please

6. **Il dit qu'il t'a vu**
   He says (that) he saw you
   **Est-ce qu'elle sait que vous êtes là?**
   Does she know that you're here?

7. **Quand tu seras plus grand et que tu auras une maison à toi, ...**
   When you're older and you have a house of your own, ...
   **Comme il pleuvait et que je n'avais pas de parapluie, ...**
   As it was raining and I didn't have an umbrella, ...

8. **Ils n'y vont pas aussi souvent que nous**
   They don't go there as often as we do
   **Il les aime plus que jamais**
   He likes them more than ever
   **L'argent est moins lourd que le plomb**
   Silver is lighter than lead

9. **Ceux-ci sont plus rares, aussi coûtent-ils cher**
   These ones are rarer, so they're expensive

## ▢ Word Order

Word order in French is largely the same as in English, except for the following. Most of these have already been dealt with under the appropriate part of speech, but are summarized here along with other instances not covered elsewhere.

- Object pronouns nearly always come before the verb → 1
  For details, see pp 166 to 170

- Certain adjectives come after the noun → 2
  For details, see p 162

- Adverbs accompanying a verb in a simple tense usually follow the verb → 3
  For details, see p 200

- After **aussi** *so, therefore*, **à peine** *hardly*, **peut-être** *perhaps*, the verb and subject are inverted → 4

- After the relative pronoun **dont** *whose* → 5
  For details, see p 182

- In exclamations, **que** and **comme** do not affect the normal word order → 6

- Following direct speech:
  – the *verb + subject* order is inverted to become *subject + verb* → 7
  – with a pronoun subject, the verb and pronoun are linked by a hyphen → 8
  – when the verb ends in a vowel in the 3rd person singular, **-t-** is inserted between the pronoun and the verb → 9

For word order in negative sentences, see p 216.
For word order in interrogative sentences, see pp 220 and 222.

# Examples

1. **Je les vois!**
   I can see them!

   **Il me l'a donné**
   He gave it to me

2. **une ville française**
   a French town

   **du vin rouge**
   some red wine

3. **Il pleut encore**
   It's still raining

   **Elle m'aide quelquefois**
   She sometimes helps me

4. **Il vit tout seul, aussi fait-il ce qu'il veut**
   He lives alone, so he does what he likes

   **À peine la pendule avait-elle sonné trois heures que …**
   Hardly had the clock struck three when …

   **Peut-être avez-vous raison**
   Perhaps you're right

5. Compare: **un homme dont je connais la fille**
   a man whose daughter I know

   and: **un homme dont la fille me connaît**
   a man whose daughter knows me

   If the person (or object) 'owned' is the *object* of the verb, the order is:

   **dont** + verb + noun (1st sentence)

   If the person (or object) 'owned' is the *subject* of the verb, the order is:

   **dont** + noun + verb (2nd sentence)

   Note also: **l'homme dont elle est la fille**
   the man whose daughter she is

6. **Qu'il fait chaud!**
   How warm it is!

   **Que je suis content de vous voir!**
   How pleased I am to see you!

   **Comme c'est cher!**
   How expensive it is!

   **Que tes voisins sont gentils!**
   How kind your neighbours are!

7. **'Je pense que oui' a dit Luc**
   ' I think so', said Luke

   **'Ça ne fait rien' répondit Jean**
   'It doesn't matter', John replied

8. **'Quelle horreur!' me suis-je exclamé**
   'How awful!' I exclaimed

9. **'Pourquoi pas?' a-t-elle demandé**
   'Why not?' she asked

   **'Si c'est vrai', continua-t-il '…'**
   'If it's true', he went on '…'

## ❑ Negatives

| | |
|---|---|
| ne ... **pas** | *not* |
| ne ... **point** (literary) | *not* |
| ne ... **rien** | *nothing* |
| ne ... **personne** | *nobody* |
| ne ... **plus** | *no longer, no more* |
| ne ... **jamais** | *never* |
| ne ... **que** | *only* |
| ne ... **aucun(e)** | *no* |
| ne ... **nul(le)** | *no* |
| ne ... **nulle part** | *nowhere* |
| ne ... **ni** | *neither ... nor* |
| ne ... **ni ... ni** | *neither ... nor* |

+ **Word order**

  – In simple tenses and the imperative:
  **ne** precedes the verb (and any object pronouns) and the second
  element follows the verb → 1

  – In compound tenses:

  i      **ne ... pas, ne ... point, ne ... rien, ne ... plus, ne ... jamais,
  ne... guère** follow the pattern:
  **ne** + auxiliary verb + **pas** + past participle → 2

  ii     **ne ... personne, ne ... que, ne ... aucun(e), ne ... nul(le),
  ne ... nulle part, ne ... ni (... ni)** follow the pattern:
  **ne** + auxiliary verb + past participle + **personne** → 3

  – With a verb in the infinitive:
  **ne ... pas, ne ... point** (*etc* see i above) come together → 4

+ For use of **rien**, **personne** and **aucun** as pronouns, see p 178.

1. **Je ne fume pas**
I don't smoke
**Ne changez rien**
Don't change anything
**Je ne vois personne**
I can't see anybody
**Nous ne nous verrons plus**
We won't see each other any more
**Il n'arrive jamais à l'heure**
He never arrives on time
**Il n'avait qu'une valise**
He only had one suitcase
**Je n'ai reçu aucune réponse**
I have received no reply
**Il ne boit ni ne fume**
He neither drinks nor smokes
**Ni mon fils ni ma fille ne les connaissaient**
Neither my son nor my daughter knew them

2. **Elle n'a pas fait ses devoirs**
She hasn't done her homework
**Ne vous a-t-il rien dit?**
Didn't he say anything to you?
**Ils n'avaient jamais vu une si belle maison**
They had never seen such a beautiful house
**Tu n'as guère changé**
You've hardly changed

3. **Je n'ai parlé à personne**
I haven't spoken to anybody
**Il n'avait mangé que la moitié du repas**
He had only eaten half the meal
**Elle ne les a trouvés nulle part**
She couldn't find them anywhere
**Il ne l'avait ni vu ni entendu**
He had neither seen nor heard him

4. **Il essayait de ne pas rire**
He was trying not to laugh

❒ **Negatives** *(Continued)*

♦ Combination of negatives. These are the most common combinations of negative particles:

| | |
|---|---|
| ne ... plus jamais | → ⒈ |
| ne ... plus personne | → ⒉ |
| ne ... plus rien | → ⒊ |
| ne ... plus ni ... ni ... | → ⒋ |
| ne ... jamais personne | → ⒌ |
| ne ... jamais rien | → ⒍ |
| ne ... jamais que | → ⒎ |
| ne ... jamais ni ... ni ... | → ⒏ |
| (ne ... pas) non plus | → ⒐ |

**non** and **pas**

♦ **non** *no* is the usual negative response to a question → ⒑
  It is often translated as *not* → ⒒

♦ **pas** is generally used when a distinction is being made, or for emphasis → ⒓
  It is often translated as *not* → ⒔

# Examples

1. **Je ne le ferai plus jamais**
   I'll never do it again

2. **Je ne connais plus personne à Rouen**
   I don't know anybody in Rouen any more

3. **Ces marchandises ne valaient plus rien**
   Those goods were no longer worth anything

4. **Ils n'ont plus ni chats ni chiens**
   They no longer have either cats or dogs

5. **On n'y voit jamais personne**
   You never see anybody there

6. **Ils ne font jamais rien d'intéressant**
   They never do anything interesting

7. **Je n'ai jamais parlé qu'à sa femme**
   I've only ever spoken to his wife

8. **Il ne m'a jamais ni écrit ni téléphoné**
   He has never either written to me or phoned me

9. **Ils n'ont pas d'enfants et nous non plus**
   They don't have any children and neither do we

   **Je ne les aime pas – Moi non plus**
   I don't like them – Neither do I/I don't either

10. **Vous voulez nous accompagner? – Non**
    Do you want to come with us? – No (I don't)

11. **Tu viens ou non?**
    Are you coming or not?

    **J'espère que non**
    I hope not

12. **Ma sœur aime le ski, moi pas**
    My sister likes skiing, I don't

13. **Qui a fait ça! – Pas moi!**
    Who did that? – Not me!

    **Est-il de retour? – Pas encore**
    Is he back? – Not yet

    **Tu as froid? – Pas du tout**
    Are you cold? – Not at all

◻ **Question forms: direct**

There are four ways of forming direct questions in French:

- by inverting the normal word order so that *pronoun subject + verb* → *verb + pronoun subject*. A hyphen links the verb and pronoun → ①

  – When the subject is a noun, a pronoun is inserted after the verb and linked to it by a hyphen → ②

  – When the verb ends in a vowel in the third person singular, **-t-** is inserted before the pronoun → ③

- by maintaining the word order *subject + verb*, but by using a rising intonation at the end of the sentence → ④

- by inserting **est-ce que** before the construction *subject + verb* → ⑤

- by using an interrogative word at the beginning of the sentence, together with inversion *or* the **est-ce que** form above → ⑥

1. **Aimez-vous la France?**
   Do you like France?
   **Est-ce possible?**
   Is it possible?
   **Part-on tout de suite?**
   Are we leaving right away?

   **Avez-vous fini?**
   Have you finished?
   **Est-elle restée?**
   Did she stay?

2. **Tes parents sont-ils en vacances?**
   Are your parents on holiday?
   **Jean-Benoît est-il parti?**
   Has Jean-Benoît left?

3. **A-t-elle de l'argent?**
   Has she any money?
   **La pièce dure-t-elle longtemps?**
   Does the play last long?
   **Mon père a-t-il téléphoné?**
   Has my father phoned?

4. **Il l'a fini**
   He's finished it
   **Robert va venir**
   Robert's coming

   **Il l'a fini?**
   Has he finished it?
   **Robert va venir?**
   Is Robert coming?

5. **Est-ce que tu la connais?**
   Do you know her?
   **Est-ce que tes parents sont revenus d'Italie?**
   Have your parents come back from Italy?

6. **Quel train** { **prends-tu?**
               { **est-ce que tu prends?**
   What train are you getting?

   **Lequel** { **est-ce que ta sœur préfère?**
           { **ta sœur préfère-t-elle?**
   Which one does your sister prefer?

   **Quand** { **êtes-vous arrivé?**
           { **est-ce que vous êtes arrivé?**
   When did you arrive?

   **Pourquoi** { **ne sont-ils pas venus?**
              { **est-ce qu'ils ne sont pas venus?**
   Why haven't they come?

## ◻ Question forms: indirect

An indirect question is one that is 'reported', e.g. he asked me *what the time was*, tell me *which way to go*. Word order in indirect questions is as follows:

- *interrogative word* + subject + verb → 1

- when the subject is a noun, and not a pronoun, the subject and verb are often inverted → 2

## ◻ n'est-ce pas

This is used wherever English would use *isn't it?, don't they?, weren't we?, is it?* etc tagged on to the end of a sentence → 3

## ◻ oui and si

**Oui** is the word for *yes* in answer to a question put in the affirmative → 4

**Si** is the word for *yes* in answer to a question put in the negative or to contradict a negative statement → 5

1. **Je me demande s'il viendra**
   I wonder if he'll come
   **Je ne sais pas à quoi ça sert**
   I don't know what it's for
   **Dites-moi quel autobus va à la gare**
   Tell me which bus goes to the station
   **Il m'a demandé combien d'argent j'avais**
   He asked me how much money I had

2. **Elle ne sait pas à quelle heure commence le film**
   She doesn't know what time the film starts
   **Je me demande où sont mes clés**
   I wonder where my keys are
   **Elle nous a demandé comment allait notre père**
   She asked us how our father was
   **Je ne sais pas ce que veulent dire ces mots**
   I don't know what these words mean

3. **Il fait chaud, n'est-ce pas?**
   It's warm, isn't it?
   **Vous n'oublierez pas, n'est-ce pas?**
   You won't forget, will you?

4. **Tu l'as fait? – Oui**
   Have you done it? – Yes (I have)

5. **Tu ne l'as pas fait? – Si**
   Haven't you done it? – Yes (I have)

```
4 6 2
8 1 5
9 3 1
```

| Cardinal | | Ordinal | |
|---|---|---|---|
| *(one, two etc)* | | *(first, second etc)* | |
| zéro | 0 | | |
| un (une) | 1 | premier (première) | 1er, 1ère |
| deux | 2 | deuxième, second(e) | 2ème |
| trois | 3 | troisième | 3ème |
| quatre | 4 | quatrième | 4ème |
| cinq | 5 | cinquième | 5ème |
| six | 6 | sixième | 6ème |
| sept | 7 | septième | 7ème |
| huit | 8 | huitième | 8ème |
| neuf | 9 | neuvième | 9ème |
| dix | 10 | dixième | 10ème |
| onze | 11 | onzième | 11ème |
| douze | 12 | douzième | 12ème |
| treize | 13 | treizième | 13ème |
| quatorze | 14 | quatorzième | 14ème |
| quinze | 15 | quinzième | 15ème |
| seize | 16 | seizième | 16ème |
| dix-sept | 17 | dix-septième | 17ème |
| dix-huit | 18 | dix-huitième | 18ème |
| dix-neuf | 19 | dix-neuvième | 19ème |
| vingt | 20 | vingtième | 20ème |
| vingt et un (une) | 21 | vingt et unième | 21ème |
| vingt-deux | 22 | vingt-deuxième | 22ème |
| vingt-trois | 23 | vingt-troisième | 23ème |
| trente | 30 | trentième | 30ème |
| quarante | 40 | quarantième | 40ème |
| cinquante | 50 | cinquantième | 50ème |
| soixante | 60 | soixantième | 60ème |
| soixante-dix | 70 | soixante-dixième | 70ème |
| soixante et onze | 71 | soixante-onzième | 71ème |
| soixante-douze | 72 | soixante-douzième | 72ème |
| quatre-vingts | 80 | quatre-vingtième | 80ème |
| quatre-vingt-un (une) | 81 | quatre-vingt-unième | 81ème |
| quatre-vingt-dix | 90 | quatre-vingt-dixième | 90ème |
| quatre-vingt-onze | 91 | quatre-vingt-onzième | 91ème |

NUMBERS

| 4 6 2 |
|---|
| 8 1 5 |
| 9 3 1 |

## Cardinal

| | |
|---|---|
| cent | 100 |
| cent un (une) | 101 |
| cent deux | 102 |
| cent dix | 110 |
| cent quarante-deux | 142 |
| deux cents | 200 |
| deux cent un (une) | 201 |
| deux cent deux | 202 |
| trois cents | 300 |
| quatre cents | 400 |
| cinq cents | 500 |
| six cents | 600 |
| sept cents | 700 |
| huit cents | 800 |
| neuf cents | 900 |
| mille | 1000 |
| mille un (une) | 1001 |
| mille deux | 1002 |
| deux mille | 2000 |
| cent mille | 100.000 |
| un million | 1.000.000 |
| deux millions | 2.000.000 |

## Ordinal

| | |
|---|---|
| centième | 100ème |
| cent unième | 101ème |
| cent deuxième | 102ème |
| cent dixième | 110ème |
| cent quarante-deuxième | 142ème |
| deux centième | 200ème |
| deux cent unième | 201ème |
| deux cent-deuxième | 202ème |
| trois centième | 300ème |
| quatre centième | 400ème |
| cinq centième | 500ème |
| six centième | 600ème |
| sept centième | 700ème |
| huit centième | 800ème |
| neuf centième | 900ème |
| millième | 1000ème |
| mille unième | 1001ème |
| mille deuxième | 1002ème |
| deux millième | 2000ème |
| cent millième | 100.000ème |
| millionième | 1.000.000ème |
| deux millionième | 2.000.000ème |

## Fractions

| | |
|---|---|
| un demi, une demie | a half |
| un tiers | a third |
| deux tiers | two thirds |
| un quart | a quarter |
| trois quarts | three quarters |
| un cinquième | one fifth |
| cinq et trois quarts | |
| five and three quarters | |

## Others

| | |
|---|---|
| zéro virgule cinq (0,5) | 0.5 |
| un virgule trois (1,3) | 1.3 |
| dix pour cent | 10% |
| deux plus deux | 2 + 2 |
| deux moins deux | 2 - 2 |
| deux fois deux | 2 x 2 |
| deux divisé par deux | 2 ÷ 2 |

⚠ NOTE the use of points with large numbers and commas with fractions, i.e. the opposite of English usage.

```
4 6 2
8 1 5
9 3 1
```
NUMBERS 226

## ◻ Other Uses

- **-aine** denoting approximate numbers:

| | |
|---|---|
| **une douzaine (de pommes)** | about a dozen (apples) |
| **une quinzaine (d'hommes)** | about fifteen (men) |
| **des centaines de personnes** | hundreds of people |
| BUT: **un millier (de voitures)** | about a thousand (cars) |

- measurements:

| | |
|---|---|
| **vingt mètres carrés** | 20 square metres |
| **vingt mètres cubes** | 20 cubic metres |
| **un pont long de quarante mètres** | a bridge 40 metres long |
| **avoir trois mètres de large/de haut** | to be 3 metres wide/ high |

- miscellaneous:

| | |
|---|---|
| **Il habite au dix** | He lives at number 10 |
| **C'est au chapitre sept** | It's in chapter 7 |
| **(C'est) à la page 17** | (It's) on page 17 |
| **(Il habite) au septième étage** | (He lives) on the 7th floor |
| **Il est arrivé le septième** | He came in 7th |
| **échelle au vingt-cinq millième** | scale 1:25,000 |

**Telephone numbers**

**Je voudrais Édimbourg trois cent trente, vingt-deux, dix**
I would like Edinburgh 330 2210
**Je voudrais le soixante-cinq, treize, vingt-deux, zéro deux**
Could you get me 65 13 22 02
**Poste trois cent trente-cinq**
Extension number 335
**Poste vingt-deux, trente-trois**
Extension number 2233

⚠ NOTE In French, telephone numbers are broken down into groups of two or three numbers (never four), and are not spoken separately as in English. They are also written in groups of two or three numbers.

## ❑ Dates

| | |
|---|---|
| **Quelle est la date d'aujourd'hui?**<br>**Quel jour sommes-nous?** } | What's the date today? |

| | |
|---|---|
| **C'est ...**<br>**Nous sommes ...** } | It's the ... |
| **le premier février** | 1st of February |
| **le deux février** | 2nd of February |
| **le vingt-huit février** | 28th of February |

**Il vient le sept mars** — He's coming on the 7th of March

⚠ NOTE Use cardinal numbers except for the first of the month.

## ❑ Years

**Je suis né en 1971** — I was born in 1971

**le douze février** { **dix-neuf cent soixante et onze**<br>**mil neuf cent soixante et onze**<br>(on) 12th February 1971

⚠ NOTE There are two ways of expressing the year (see last example).
Note the spelling of **mil** *one thousand* in dates.

## ❑ Other expressions

| | |
|---|---|
| **dans les années cinquante** | during the fifties |
| **au vingtième siècle** | in the twentieth century |
| **en mai** | in May |
| **lundi (quinze)** | on Monday (the 15th) |
| **le lundi** | on Mondays |
| **dans dix jours** | in 10 days' time |
| **il y a dix jours** | 10 days ago |

**Quelle heure est-il?**  *What time is it?*
**Il est ...**  *It's ...*

| | | |
|---|---|---|
| 00.00 | **minuit** *midnight, twelve o'clock* | |
| 00.10 | **minuit dix, zéro heure dix** | |
| 00.15 | **minuit et quart, zéro heure quinze** | |
| 00.30 | **minuit et demi, zéro heure trente** | |
| 00.45 | **une heure moins (le) quart, zéro heure quarante-cinq** | |

| | |
|---|---|
| 01.00 | **une heure du matin** *one a.m., one o'clock in the morning* |
| 01.10 | **une heure dix (du matin)** |
| 01.15 | **une heure et quart, une heure quinze** |
| 01.30 | **une heure et demie, une heure trente** |
| 01.45 | **deux heures moins (le) quart, une heure quarante-cinq** |
| 01.50 | **deux heures moins dix, une heure cinquante** |
| 01.59 | **deux heures moins une, une heure cinquante-neuf** |

| | |
|---|---|
| 12.00 | **midi, douze heures** *noon, twelve o'clock* |
| 12.30 | **midi et demi, douze heures trente** |

| | |
|---|---|
| 13.00 | **une heure de l'après-midi, treize heures** *one p.m., one o'clock in the afternoon* |
| 01.30 | **une heure et demie (de l'après-midi), treize heures trente** |

| | |
|---|---|
| 19.00 | **sept heures du soir, dix-neuf heures** *seven p.m., seven o'clock in the evening* |
| 19.30 | **sept heures et demie (du soir), dix-neuf heures trente** |

**À quelle heure venez-vous? – À sept heures**
What time are you coming? – At seven o'clock
**Les bureaux sont fermés de midi à quatorze heures**
The offices are closed from twelve until two
**à deux heures du matin/de l'après-midi**
at two o'clock in the morning/afternoon, at two a.m./p.m.
**à sept heures du soir**
at seven o'clock in the evening, at seven p.m.
**à cinq heures précises** or **pile**
at five o'clock sharp
**vers neuf heures**
about nine o'clock
**peu avant/après midi**
shortly before/after noon
**entre huit et neuf heures**
between eight and nine o'clock
**Il est plus de trois heures et demie**
It's after half past three
**Il faut y être à dix heures au plus tard/au plus tôt**
You have to be there by ten o'clock at the latest/earliest
**Ne venez pas plus tard que onze heures moins le quart**
Come no later than a quarter to eleven
**Il en a pour une demi-heure**
He'll be half an hour (at it)
**Elle est restée sans connaissance pendant un quart d'heure**
She was unconscious for a quarter of an hour
**Je les attends depuis une heure**
I've been waiting for them for an hour/since one o'clock
**Ils sont partis il y a quelques minutes**
They left a few minutes ago
**Je l'ai fait en vingt minutes**
I did it in twenty minutes
**Le train arrive dans une heure**
The train arrives in an hour('s time)
**Combien de temps dure ce film?**
How long does this film last?

Beware of translating word for word. While on occasion this is quite possible, quite often it is not. The need for caution is illustrated by the following:

- English phrasal verbs (i.e. verbs followed by a preposition) e.g. *to run away*, *to fall down* are often translated by one word in French → [1]

- English verbal constructions often contain a preposition where none exists in French, or vice versa → [2]

- Two or more prepositions in English may have a single rendering in French → [3]

- A word which is singular in English may be plural in French, or vice versa → [4]

- French has no equivalent of the possessive construction denoted by --'s/--s' → [5]

See also *at/in/to*, p 234.

**Specific problems**

**-ing**

This is translated in a variety of ways in French:

- *to be …-ing* is translated by a simple verb → [6]
  EXCEPTION: when a physical position is denoted, a past participle is used → [7]

- in the construction *to see/hear sb …-ing*, use an infinitive or **qui** + verb → [8]

*-ing* can also be translated by:
  – an infinitive → [9] (see p 44)

  – a perfect infinitive → [10] (see p 46)

  – a present participle → [11] (see p 48)

  – a noun → [12]

*Grammar*

| | | |
|---|---|---|
| **1** | **s'enfuir** | **tomber** | **céder** |
| | to run away | to fall down | to give in |
| **2** | **payer** | **regarder** | **écouter** |
| | to pay for | to look at | to listen to |
| | **obéir à** | **nuire à** | **manquer de** |
| | to obey | to harm | to lack |
| **3** | **s'étonner de** | | **satisfait de** |
| | to be surprised at | | satisfied with |
| | **voler qch à** | | **apte à** |
| | to steal sth from | | capable of; fit for |
| **4** | **les bagages** | | **ses cheveux** |
| | the luggage | | his/her hair |
| | **le bétail** | | **mon pantalon** |
| | the cattle | | my trousers |
| **5** | **la voiture de mon frère** | | **la chambre des enfants** |
| | my brother's car | | the children's bedroom |
| | *(literally: ... of my brother)* | | *(literally: ... of the children)* |
| **6** | **Il part demain** | | **Je lisais un roman** |
| | He's leaving tomorrow | | I was reading a novel |
| **7** | **Elle est assise là-bas** | | **Il était couché par terre** |
| | She's sitting over there | | He was lying on the ground |

**8**   **Je les vois** { **venir** / **qui viennent** } I can see them coming

     **Je l'ai entendue** { **chanter** / **qui chantait** } I heard her singing

| | | |
|---|---|---|
| **9** | **J'aime aller au cinéma** | **Arrêtez de parler!** |
| | I like going to the cinema | Stop talking! |
| | **Au lieu de répondre** | **Avant de partir** |
| | Instead of answering | Before leaving |
| **10** | **Après avoir ouvert la boîte, il ...** | |
| | After opening the box, he ... | |
| **11** | **Étant plus timide que moi, elle ...** | |
| | Being shyer than me, she ... | |
| **12** | **Le ski me maintient en forme** | |
| | Skiing keeps me fit | |

**to be**

- Generally translated by **être** → ☐ 1
  When physical location is implied, **se trouver** may be used → ☐ 2

- In set expressions, describing physical and emotional conditions, **avoir** is used:

| | |
|---|---|
| **avoir chaud/froid** | to be warm/cold |
| **avoir faim/soif** | to be hungry/thirsty |
| **avoir peur/honte** | to be afraid/ashamed |
| **avoir tort/raison** | to be wrong/right |

- Describing the weather, e.g. *what's the weather like?, it's windy/sunny*, use **faire** → ☐ 3

- For ages, e.g. *he is 6*, use **avoir** → ☐ 4

- For state of health, e.g. *he's unwell, how are you?*, use **aller** → ☐ 5

**it is, it's**

- Usually **il/elle est**, when referring to a noun → ☐ 6

- For expressions of time, also use **il est** → ☐ 7

- To describe the weather, e.g. *it's windy*, see above.

- In the construction: *it is difficult/easy to do sth*, use **il est** → ☐ 8

- In all other constructions, use **c'est** → ☐ 9

**there is/there are**

- Both are translated by **il y a** → ☐ 10

**can, be able**

- Physical ability is expressed by **pouvoir** → ☐ 11

- If the meaning is *to know how to*, use **savoir** → ☐ 12

- *Can* + a 'verb of hearing or seeing etc' in English is not translated in French → ☐ 13

1. **Il est tard**      **C'est peu probable**
   It's late      It's not very likely

2. **Où se trouve la gare?**
   Where's the station?

3. **Quel temps fait-il?**      **Il fait beau/mauvais/du vent**
   What's the weather like?      It's lovely/miserable/windy

4. **Quel âge avez-vous?**      **J'ai quinze ans**
   How old are you?      I'm fifteen

5. **Comment allez-vous?**      **Je vais très bien**
   How are you?      I'm very well

6. **Où est mon parapluie? – Il est là, dans le coin**
   Where's my umbrella? – It's there, in the corner
   **Descends la valise si elle n'est pas trop lourde**
   Bring down the case if it isn't too heavy

7. **Quelle heure est-il? – Il est sept heures et demie**
   What's the time? – It's half past seven

8. **Il est difficile de répondre à cette question**
   It's difficult to reply to this question

9. **C'est moi qui ne l'aime pas**
   It's me who doesn't like him
   **C'est Charles/ma mère qui l'a dit**
   It's Charles/my mother who said so
   **C'est ici que je les ai achetés**
   It's here that I bought them
   **C'est parce que la poste est fermée que …**
   It's because the post office is closed that …

10. **Il y a quelqu'un à la porte**
    There's somebody at the door
    **Il y a cinq livres sur la table**
    There are five books on the table

11. **Pouvez-vous atteindre cette étagère?**
    Can you reach up to that shelf?

12. **Elle ne sait pas nager**
    She can't swim

13. **Je ne vois rien**      **Il les entendait**
    I can't see anything      He could hear them

**to** (see also below)

- Generally translated by **à** → ①
  (See p 204).

- In time expressions, e.g. *10 to 6*, use **moins** → ②

- When the meaning is *in order to*, use **pour** → ③

- Following a verb, as in *to try to do, to like to do*, see pp 44 and 64

- *easy/difficult/impossible etc to do:*
  The preposition used depends on whether a specific noun is referred
  to → ④ or not → ⑤

## at/in/to

- With feminine countries, use **en** → ⑥
  With masculine countries, use **au** (**aux** with plural countries) → ⑦

- With towns, use **à** → ⑧

- *at/to the butcher's/grocer's etc*: use **à** + noun designating the
  shop, or **chez** + noun designating the shopkeeper → ⑨

- *at/to the dentist's/doctor's etc*: use **chez** → ⑩

- *at/to ...'s/...s' house*: use **chez** → ⑪

1. **Donne le livre à Patrick**
   Give the book to Patrick

2. **dix heures moins cinq**       **à sept heures moins le quart**
   five to ten                   at a quarter to seven

3. **Je l'ai fait pour vous aider**
   I did it to help you

   **Il se pencha pour nouer son lacet**
   He bent down to tie his shoelace

4. **Ce livre est difficile à lire**
   This book is difficult to read

5. **Il est difficile de comprendre leurs raisons**
   It's difficult to understand their reasons

6. **Il est allé en France/en Suisse**
   He has gone to France/to Switzerland

   **un village en Norvège/en Belgique**
   a village in Norway/in Belgium

7. **Êtes-vous allé au Canada/au Danemark/aux États-Unis?**
   Have you been to Canada/to Denmark/to the United States?

   **une ville au Japon/au Brésil**
   a town in Japan/in Brazil

8. **Il est allé à Vienne/à Bruxelles**
   He has gone to Vienna/to Brussels

   **Il habite à Londres/à Genève**
   He lives in London/in Geneva

   **Ils logent dans un hôtel à St. Pierre**
   They're staying in a hotel at St. Pierre

9. **Je l'ai acheté** { **à l'épicerie** / **chez l'épicier** }    I bought it at the grocer's

   **Elle est allée** { **à la boulangerie** / **chez le boulanger** }    She's gone to the baker's

10. **J'ai un rendez-vous chez le dentiste**
    I've an appointment at the dentist's

    **Il est allé chez le médecin**
    He has gone to the doctor's

11. **chez Christian**             **chez les Pagot**
    at/to Christian's house     at/to the Pagots' house

## ❏ General Points

◆ **Activity of the lips**

The lips play a very important part in French. When a vowel is described as having 'rounded' lips, the lips are slightly drawn together and pursed, as when an English speaker expresses exaggerated surprise with the vowel 'ooh!' Equally, if the lips are said to be 'spread', the corners are pulled firmly back towards the cheeks, tending to reveal the front teeth.

In English, lip position is not important, and vowel sounds tend to merge because of this. In French, the activity of the lips means that every vowel sound is clearly distinct from every other.

◆ **No diphthongs**

A diphthong is a glide between two vowel sounds in the same syllable. In English, there are few 'pure' vowel sounds, but largely diphthongs instead. Although speakers of English may *think they* produce one vowel sound in the word 'day', in fact they use a diphthong, which in this instance is a glide between the vowels [e] and [ɪ]: [deɪ]. In French the tension maintained in the lips, tongue and the mouth in general prevents diphthongs occurring, as the vowel sound is kept constant throughout. Hence the French word corresponding to the above example, 'dé', is pronounced with no final [ɪ] sound, but is phonetically represented thus: [de].

◆ **Consonants**

In English, consonants are often pronounced with a degree of laxness that can result in their practically disappearing altogether although not strictly 'silent'. In a relaxed pronunciation of a word such as 'hat', the 't' is often scarcely heard, or is replaced by a 'glottal stop' (a sort of jerk in the throat). This never occurs in French, where consonants are always given their full value.

## ◻ Pronunciation of Consonants

Some consonants are pronounced almost exactly as in English: [b, p, f, v, g, k, m, w].

Most others are similar to English, but slight differences should be noted.

| EXAMPLES | HINTS ON PRONUNCIATION |
|---|---|
| [d] **d**inde | |
| [t] **t**ente | The tip of the tongue touches the upper front |
| [n] **n**o**nn**e | teeth and not the roof of the mouth as in English |
| [l] **L**i**ll**e | |
| [s] tou**s ç**a | The tip of the tongue is down behind the |
| [z] **z**éro ro**s**e | bottom front teeth, lower than in English |
| [ʃ] **ch**ose ta**ch**e | Like the *sh* of English *shout* |
| [ʒ] **j**e **g**ilet bei**g**e | Like the *s* of English *measure* |
| [j] **y**eux pai**ll**e | Like the *y* of English *yes* |

Three consonants are not heard in English:

| | |
|---|---|
| [ʀ] **r**a**r**e veni**r** | R is often silent in English, e.g. fa**r**m. In French the [ʀ] is never silent, unless it follows an **e** at the end of a word e.g. cherch**er**. To pronounce it, try to make a short sound like gargling. Similar, too, to the Scottish pronunciation of *loch* |
| [ɲ] vi**gn**e a**gn**eau | Similar to the *ni* of Span**i**ard |
| [ɥ] h**u**ile l**u**eur | Like a very rapid [y] (see p 239) followed immediately by the next vowel of the word |

## ◻ Pronunciation of Vowels

| | EXAMPLES | HINTS ON PRONUNCIATION |
|---|---|---|
| [a] | patte plat amour | Similar to the vowel in English *pat* |
| [ɑ] | bas pâte | Longer than the sound above, it resembles the English exclamation of surprise *ah!* Similar, too, to the English vowel in *car* without the final *r* sound |
| [ɛ] | lait jouet merci | Similar to the English vowel in *pet*. Beware of using the English diphthong [eɪ] as in *pay* |
| [e] | été jouer | A pure vowel, again quite different from the diphthong in English *pay* |
| [ə] | le premier | Similar to the English sound in *butter* when the *r* is not pronounced |
| [i] | ici vie lycee | The lips are well spread towards the cheeks while uttering this sound. Shorter than the English vowel in *see* |
| [ɔ] | mort homme | The lips are well rounded while producing a sound similar to the *o* of English *cot* |
| [o] | mot dôme eau | A pure vowel with strongly rounded lips quite different from the diphthong in English *bone*, *low* |

| | | |
|---|---|---|
| [u] | gen**ou** r**ou**e | A pure vowel with strongly rounded lips. Similar to the English *ooh!* of surprise |
| [y] | r**u**e v**ê**tu | Often the most difficult for English speakers to produce: round your lips and try to pronounce [i] (see above). There is no [j] sound (see p 237) as there is in English *pure* |
| [œ] | s**œu**r b**eu**rre | Similar to the vowel in English *fir* or *murmur*, but without the *r* sound and with the lips more strongly rounded |
| [ø] | p**eu** d**eu**x | To pronounce this, try to say [e] (see above) with the lips strongly rounded |

**Nasal Vowels**

These are spelt with a vowel followed by a 'nasal' consonant – **n** or **m**. The production of nasal vowels really requires the help of a teacher or a recording of the sound. However, to help you, the vowel is pronounced by allowing the air from the lungs to come partly down the nose and partly through the mouth, and the **n** or **m** is not pronounced at all.

| | | |
|---|---|---|
| [ɑ̃] | l**en**t s**an**g d**an**s | In each case, the vowel shown in the phonetic symbol is pronounced as described above, but air is allowed to come through the nose as well as the mouth |
| [ɛ̃] | mat**in** pl**ein** | |
| [ɔ̃] | n**on** p**on**t | |
| [œ̃] | br**un** **un** parf**um** | |

## ◻ From Spelling to Sounds

Although it may not seem so at first sight, there are some fairly precise 'rules' which can help you to know how to pronounce French words from their spelling.

### Vowels

| SPELLING | PRONOUNCED | EXAMPLES |
|---|---|---|
| **a, à** | [a] | chatte, table |
| **a, â** | [ɑ] | pâte, pas |
| **e, é** | [e] | été, marcher |
| **e, é, ê** | [ɛ] | fenêtre, fermer, chère |
| **e** | [ə] | double, fenêtre |
| **i, î, y** | [i] | lit, abîmer, lycée |
| **o, ô** | [o] | pot, trop, dôme |
| **o** | [ɔ] | sotte, orange |
| **u, û** | [y] | battu, fût, pur |

### Vowel Groups

There are several groups of vowels in French spelling which are regularly pronounced in the same way:

| | | |
|---|---|---|
| **ai** | [ɛ] or [e] | maison, marchai, faire |
| **ail** | [aj] | portail |
| **ain, aim, (c)in, im** | [ɛ̃] | pain, faim, frein, impair |
| **au** | [o] | auberge, landau |
| **an, am, en, em** | [ɑ̃] | plan, ample, entrer, temps |
| **eau** | [o] | bateau, eau |
| **eu** | [œ] or [ø] | feu, peur |
| **euil(le), ueil** | [œj] | feuille, recueil |
| **oi, oy** | [wa] | voire, voyage |
| **on, om** | [ɔ̃] | ton, compter |
| **ou** | [u] | hibou, outil |
| **œu** | [œ] | sœur, cœur |
| **ue** | [y] | rue |
| **un, um** | [œ̃] | brun, parfum |

Added to these are the many groups of letters occurring at the end of words, where their pronunciation is predictable, bearing in mind the tendency (see p 242) of final consonants to remain silent:

| TYPICAL WORDS | PRONUNCIATION OF FINAL SYLLABLE |
|---|---|
| **pas, mât, chat** | [ɑ] or [a] |
| **marcher, marchez, marchais, marchait, baie, valet, mes, fumée** | [e] or [ε] |
| **nid** | [i] |
| **chaud, vaut, faux, sot, tôt, Pernod, dos, croc** | [o] |
| **bout, bijoux, sous, boue** | [u] |
| **fut, fût, crus, crûs** | [y] |
| **queue, heureux, bleus** | [ø] |
| **en, vend, vent, an, sang, grand, dans** | [ɑ̃] |
| **fin, feint, frein, vain** | [ε̃] |
| **on, pont, fond, avons** | [ɔ̃] |
| **brun, parfum** | [œ̃] |

## ❏ From Spelling to Sounds *(Continued)*

### Consonants

♦ Final consonants are usually silent → ⚊1⚊

♦ **n** or **m** at the end of a syllable or word are silent, but they have the effect of 'nasalizing' the preceding vowel(s) (see p 239 on Nasal Vowels)

♦ The letter **h** is either 'silent' ('mute') or 'aspirate' when it begins a word. When silent, the word behaves as though it started with a vowel and takes a liaison with the preceding word where appropriate.

When the **h** is aspirate, no liaison is made → ⚊2⚊

There is no way of predicting which words start with which sort of **h** – this simply has to be learnt with each word

♦ The following consonants in spelling have predictable pronunciations: b, d, f, k, l, p, r, t, v, w, x, y, z. Others vary:

| SPELLING | PRONOUNCED | ENGLISH EXAMPLES | |
|---|---|---|---|
| **c** + a, o, u | [k] | **c**an, **c**ot, **c**ut | → ⚊3⚊ |
| + l, r | | **cl**ass, **cr**am | |
| **c** + e, i, y | [s] | **c**eiling, i**c**e | → ⚊4⚊ |
| **ç** + a, o, u | [s] | **c**eiling, i**c**e | → ⚊5⚊ |
| **ch** | [ʃ] | **sh**op, la**sh** | → ⚊6⚊ |
| **g** + a, o, u | [g] | **g**ate, **g**ot, **g**un | → ⚊7⚊ |
| + l, r | | **gl**ass, **gr**amme | |
| **g** + e, i, y | [ʒ] | lei**s**ure | → ⚊8⚊ |
| **gn** | [ɲ] | compa**ni**on, o**ni**on | → ⚊9⚊ |
| **j** | [ʒ] | mea**s**ure | → ⚊10⚊ |
| **q, qu** | [k] | **qu**ay, **k**it | → ⚊11⚊ |
| **s** between vowels | [z] | ro**s**e | → ⚊12⚊ |
| elsewhere | [s] | **s**it | |
| **th** | [t] | **Th**omas | → ⚊13⚊ |
| **t** in **-tion** | [s] | **s**it | → ⚊14⚊ |

| | | | |
|---|---|---|---|
| 1 | **éclat** [ekla] | **nez** [ne] | |
| | **chaud** [ʃo] | **aider** [ede] | |
| 2 | silent **h**: | aspirate **h**: | |
| | **des hôtels** [de zotɛl] | **des haricots** [de aʀiko] | |
| 3 | **café** [kafe] | **côte** [kot] | **culture** [kyltyʀ] |
| | **classe** [klas] | **croûte** [kʀut] | |
| 4 | **ceci** [səsi] | **cil** [sil] | **cycliste** [siklist] |
| 5 | **ça** [sa] | **garçon** [gaʀsɔ̃] | **déçu** [desy] |
| 6 | **chat** [ʃa] | **riche** [ʀiʃ] | |
| 7 | **gare** [gaʀ] | **gourde** [guʀd] | **aigu** [ɛgy] |
| | **glaise** [glɛz] | **gramme** [gʀam] | |
| 8 | **gemme** [ʒem] | **gilet** [ʒilɛ] | **gymnaste** [ʒimnast] |
| 9 | **vigne** [viɲ] | **oignon** [ɔɲɔ̃] | |
| 10 | **joli** [ʒɔli] | **Jules** [ʒyl] | |
| 11 | **quiche** [kiʃ] | **quitter** [kite] | |
| 12 | **sable** [sablə] | **maison** [mɛzɔ̃] | |
| 13 | **théâtre** [teatʀ] | **Thomas** [tɔma] | |
| 14 | **nation** [nasjɔ̃] | **action** [aksjɔ̃] | |

## ◻ Feminine Forms and Pronunciation

- For adjectives and nouns ending in a vowel in the masculine, the addition of an **e** to form the feminine does not alter the pronunciation → 1

- If the masculine ends with a silent consonant, generally **-d**, **-s**, **-r** or **-t**, the consonant is sounded in the feminine → 2
  This also applies when the final consonant is doubled before the addition of the feminine **e** → 3

- If the masculine ends in a nasal vowel and a silent **n**, e.g. **-an**, **-on**, **-in**, the vowel is no longer nasalized and the **-n** is pronounced in the feminine → 4
  This also applies when the final **-n** is doubled before the addition of the feminine **e** → 5

- Where the masculine and feminine forms have totally different endings (see pp 136 and 150), the pronunciation of course varies accordingly → 6

## ◻ Plural Forms and Pronunciation

- The addition of **s** or **x** to form regular plurals generally does not affect pronunciation → 7

- Where liaison has to be made, the final **-s** or **-x** of the plural form is pronounced → 8

- Where the masculine singular and plural forms have totally different endings (see pp 138 and 148), the pronunciation of course varies accordingly → 9

- Note the change in pronunciation in the following nouns:

| SINGULAR | | PLURAL | | |
|---|---|---|---|---|
| **bœuf** | [bœf] | **bœufs** | [bø] | *ox/oxen* |
| **œuf** | [œf] | **œufs** | [ø] | *egg/eggs* |
| **os** | [ɔs] | **os** | [o] | *bone/bones* |

grammar

| | ADJECTIVES | | NOUNS | |
|---|---|---|---|---|
| 1 | joli<br>[ʒɔli] | → jolie<br>[ʒɔli] | un ami<br>[ami] | → une amie<br>[ami] |
| | déçu<br>[desy] | → déçue<br>[desy] | un employé<br>[ɑ̃plwaje] | → une employée<br>[ɑ̃plwaje] |
| 2 | chaud<br>[ʃo] | → chaude<br>[ʃod] | un étudiant<br>[etydjɑ̃] | → une étudiante<br>[etydjɑ̃t] |
| | français<br>[frɑ̃sɛ] | → française<br>[frɑ̃sɛz] | un Anglais<br>[ɑ̃glɛ] | → une Anglaise<br>[ɑ̃glɛz] |
| | inquiet<br>[ɛ̃kjɛ] | → inquiète<br>[ɛ̃kjɛt] | un étranger<br>[etrɑ̃ʒe] | → une étrangère<br>[etrɑ̃ʒɛr] |
| 3 | violet<br>[vjɔlɛ] | → violette<br>[vjɔlɛt] | le cadet<br>[kadɛ] | → la cadette<br>[kadɛt] |
| | gras<br>[grɑ] | → grasse<br>[grɑs] | | |
| 4 | plein<br>[plɛ̃] | → pleine<br>[plɛn] | le souverain<br>[suvrɛ̃] | → la souveraine<br>[suvrɛn] |
| | fin<br>[fɛ̃] | → fine<br>[fin] | Le Persan<br>[pɛrsɑ̃] | → La Persane<br>[pɛrsan] |
| | brun<br>[brœ̃] | → brune<br>[bryn] | le voisin<br>[vwazɛ̃] | → la voisine<br>[vwazin] |
| 5 | canadien<br>[kanadjɛ̃] | → canadienne<br>[kanadjɛn] | le paysan<br>[peizɑ̃] | → la paysanne<br>[peizan] |
| | breton<br>[brətɔ̃] | → bretonne<br>[brətɔn] | le baron<br>[barɔ̃] | → la baronne<br>[barɔn] |
| 6 | vif<br>[vif] | → vive<br>[viv] | le veuf<br>[vœf] | → la veuve<br>[vœv] |
| | traître<br>[trɛtrɛ] | → traîtresse<br>[trɛtrɛs] | le maître<br>[mɛtrə] | → la maîtresse<br>[mɛtrɛs] |
| 7 | beau<br>[bo] | → beaux<br>[bo] | la maison<br>[mɛzɔ̃] | → les maisons<br>[mɛzɔ̃] |
| 8 | des anciens élèves<br>[de zɑ̃sjɛ̃ zelev] | | de beaux arbres<br>[də bo zarbr(ə)] | |
| 9 | amical<br>[amikal] | → amicaux<br>[amiko] | un journal<br>[ʒurnal] | → des journaux<br>[ʒurno] |

## ⬭ The Alphabet

| | | | | | | | |
|---|---|---|---|---|---|---|---|
| **A, a** | [ɑ] | **J, j** | [ʒi] | **S, s** | [ɛs] | | |
| **B, b** | [be] | **K, k** | [ka] | **T, t** | [te] | | |
| **C, c** | [se] | **L, l** | [el] | **U, u** | [y] | | |
| **D, d** | [de] | **M, m** | [ɛm] | **V, v** | [ve] | | |
| **E, e** | [ə] | **N, n** | [ɛn] | **W, w** | [dubləve] | | |
| **F, f** | [ɛf] | **O, o** | [o] | **X, x** | [iks] | | |
| **G, g** | [ʒe] | **P, p** | [pe] | **Y, y** | [igʀɛk] | | |
| **H, h** | [aʃ] | **Q, q** | [ky] | **Z, z** | [zɛd] | | |
| **I, i** | [i] | **R, r** | [ɛʀ] | | | | |

Capital letters are used as in English except for the following:

♦ adjectives of nationality
  e.g. **une ville espagnole**      **un auteur français**
      a Spanish town              a French author

♦ languages
  e.g. **Parlez-vous anglais?**      **Il parle français et allemand**
      Do you speak English?       He speaks French and German

♦ days of the week:

| | |
|---|---|
| **lundi** | Monday |
| **mardi** | Tuesday |
| **mercredi** | Wednesday |
| **jeudi** | Thursday |
| **vendredi** | Friday |
| **samedi** | Saturday |
| **dimanche** | Sunday |

♦ months of the year:

| | | | |
|---|---|---|---|
| **janvier** | January | **juillet** | July |
| **février** | February | **août** | August |
| **mars** | March | **septembre** | September |
| **avril** | April | **octobre** | October |
| **mai** | May | **novembre** | November |
| **juin** | June | **décembre** | December |

The following index lists comprehensively both grammatical terms and key words in French and English contained in this book.